D0699530

1st EDITION

Perspectives on Modern World History

The Haiti Earthquake

1st EDITION

Perspectives on Modern World History

The Haiti Earthquake

Diane Andrews Henningfeld

Editor

GREENHAVEN PRESS
A part of Gale, Cengage Learning

Detroit • New York • San Francisco • New Haven, Conn • Waterville, Maine • London

Elizabeth Des Chenes, *Director, Publishing Solutions*

© 2013 Greenhaven Press, a part of Gale, Cengage Learning.

Gale and Greenhaven Press are registered trademarks used herein under license.

For more information, contact:
Greenhaven Press
27500 Drake Rd.
Farmington Hills, MI 48331-3535
Or you can visit our Internet site at gale.cengage.com.

For product information and technology assistance, contact us at
Gale Customer Support, 1-800-877-4253.

For permission to use material from this text or product, submit all requests online at
www.cengage.com/permissions.

Further permissions questions can be e-mailed to permissionrequest@cengage.com.

Articles in Greenhaven Press anthologies are often edited for length to meet page requirements. In addition, original titles of these works are changed to clearly present the main thesis and to explicitly indicate the author's opinion. Every effort is made to ensure that Greenhaven Press accurately reflects the original intent of the authors. Every effort has been made to trace the owners of copyrighted material.

Cover image © Reynold Mainse/Design Pics/Corbis and © Enrique Perez Huerta/Demotix/Corbis.

LIBRARY OF CONGRESS CATALOGING-IN-PUBLICATION DATA

The Haiti earthquake / Diane Andrews Henningfeld, book editor.
   p. cm. -- (Perspectives on modern world history)
   Includes bibliographical references and index.
   ISBN 978-0-7377-6367-6 (hardcover)
 1. Haiti Earthquake, Haiti, 2010--Juvenile literature. 2. Haiti Earthquake, Haiti, 2010--Sources. I. Henningfeld, Diane Andrews.
   F1928.2.H286 2012
   63.34'958097294--dc23

                                                      2012015804

Printed in the United States of America
1 2 3 4 5 6 7 16 15 14 13 12

CONTENTS

The president of the United States reports that US rescue and relief workers have arrived in Haiti to help United States and Haitian citizens in their recovery from the earthquake. He pledges ongoing help for Haiti.

the Dominican Republic without permission. Members of the group claim they were rescuing orphans; Haiti says they were engaged in child trafficking.

CHAPTER **3** Personal Narratives

tell their individual experiences in providing medical response to the victims of the Haiti earthquake.

FOREWORD

"History cannot give us a program for the future, but it can give us a fuller understanding of ourselves, and of our common humanity, so that we can better face the future."

—Robert Penn Warren, American poet and novelist

The history of each nation is punctuated by momentous events that represent turning points for that nation, with an impact felt far beyond its borders. These events—displaying the full range of human capabilities, from violence, greed, and ignorance to heroism, courage, and strength—are nearly always complicated and multifaceted. Any student of history faces the challenge of grasping the many strands that constitute such world-changing events as wars, social movements, and environmental disasters. But understanding these significant historic events can be enhanced by exposure to a variety of perspectives, whether of people involved intimately or of ones observing from a distance of miles or years. Understanding can also be increased by learning about the controversies surrounding such events and exploring hot-button issues from multiple angles. Finally, true understanding of important historic events involves knowledge of the events' human impact—of the ways such events affected people in their everyday lives—all over the world.

Perspectives on Modern World History examines global historic events from the twentieth century onward by presenting analysis and observation from numerous vantage points. Each volume offers high school, early college level, and general interest readers a thematically

1

arranged anthology of previously published materials that address a major historical event, with an emphasis on international coverage. Each volume opens with background information on the event, then presents the controversies surrounding that event, and concludes with first-person narratives from people who lived through the event or were affected by it. By providing primary sources from the time of the event, as well as relevant commentary surrounding the event, this series can be used to inform debate, help develop critical thinking skills, increase global awareness, and enhance an understanding of international perspectives on history.

Material in each volume is selected from a diverse range of sources, including journals, magazines, newspapers, nonfiction books, personal narratives, speeches, congressional testimony, government documents, pamphlets, organization newsletters, and position papers. Articles taken from these sources are carefully edited and introduced to provide context and background. Each volume of Perspectives on Modern World History includes an array of views on events of global significance. Much of the material comes from international sources and from US sources that provide extensive international coverage.

Each volume in the Perspectives on Modern World History series also includes:

- A full-color **world map**, offering context and geographic perspective.
- An annotated **table of contents** that provides a brief summary of each essay in the volume.
- An **introduction** specific to the volume topic.
- For each viewpoint, a brief **introduction** that has notes about the author and source of the viewpoint, and that provides a summary of its main points.
- Full-color **charts**, **graphs**, **maps**, and other visual representations.

- Informational **sidebars** that explore the lives of key individuals, give background on historical events, or explain scientific or technical concepts.
- A **glossary** that defines key terms, as needed.
- A **chronology** of important dates preceding, during, and immediately following the event.
- A **bibliography** of additional books, periodicals, and websites for further research.
- A comprehensive **subject index** that offers access to people, places, and events cited in the text.

Perspectives on Modern World History is designed for a broad spectrum of readers who want to learn more about not only history but also current events, political science, government, international relations, and sociology—students doing research for class assignments or debates, teachers and faculty seeking to supplement course materials, and others wanting to improve their understanding of history. Each volume of Perspectives on Modern World History is designed to illuminate a complicated event, to spark debate, and to show the human perspective behind the world's most significant happenings of recent decades.

INTRODUCTION

On January 12, 2010, at about 4:53 P.M. local time, a 7.0 magnitude earthquake hit Haiti approximately sixteen miles from Port-au-Prince, the capital city and most densely populated area of the country. Even before the earthquake, according to the *CIA World Factbook*, Haiti was "the poorest country in the Western Hemisphere with 80% of the population living under the poverty line and 54% in abject poverty." The earthquake made the situation in Haiti unspeakably worse.

The nation of Haiti is located on the eastern third of the island of Hispaniola, in the Caribbean Sea. Haiti shares the island with the Dominican Republic, comprising the remaining two-thirds of Hispaniola. Haiti is slightly smaller than the state of Maryland, although its population is nearly double.

Throughout its history, Haiti has struggled with hurricanes, famine, and political unrest. In 2008, for example, Haiti was hit by four named storms: Fay, Gustav, Hannah, and Ike. These tropical storms wiped out Haiti's agriculture, according to a 2008 Associated Press report titled "Millions in Haiti Could Face Famine after Floods." Many people perished in the floods, and many more were weakened by the subsequent famine conditions. However, the scope of the 2010 earthquake was greater than any natural disaster in the past two hundred years, according to the *CIA World Factbook*.

Within minutes of the quake, some 70 percent of the buildings in Port-au-Prince were destroyed, and thousands of residents were trapped in the wreckage. Survivors dug through the remains of buildings in the desperate hope of freeing their friends, their families, and their fellow countrymen. They worked with their hands and muscles, using flashlights after dark, as all power to the area was cut off.

The rubble presented additional problems: Not only was it difficult to free those trapped, but the rubble-blocked roadways made evacuating the injured to medical stations extraordinarily difficult. In the early hours after the quake, the only medical facility available was the Argentine Air Force mobile field hospital, which was part of a United Nations peacekeeping force already in Haiti at the time of the quake.

Search and rescue teams from multiple nations quickly organized and arrived in Haiti in subsequent days. Even with the modern equipment the teams brought, it was a formidable challenge to free survivors and recover the dead. Many died while awaiting rescue.

Food, water, and emergency medical supplies also arrived in Haiti from many nations within days of the quake. However, distributing the life-saving resources became a problem. With the infrastructure largely destroyed, reaching people desperate for food and water was difficult. Indeed, the distribution of supplies remained the single biggest problem in the days and weeks following the quake. Violence erupted at many distribution centers as people struggled to access food and water. Sadly, in addition to those truly in need of these supplies, criminal elements also contributed to the violence, stealing and looting supplies to sell on the black market to desperate residents. Three weeks after the quake, the United Nations World Food Programme chose to only give food and water to women who had vouchers for the supplies. In this way, they hoped to make sure the food and water was going to those who needed it most.

In addition, military aid from around the world, and particularly from the United States, arrived to help in the humanitarian relief effort. For the Haitians, seeing US military troops on their soil was a mixed blessing. As recently as 1994, US troops invaded Haiti to intervene in the political turmoil following the ouster of Haitian president Jean-Bertrand Aristide. The United States returned Aristide to power and maintained a military presence in Haiti for five years. This was not the first time the US military had seized internal control of Haiti. In 1915 the US began an occupation in Haiti that lasted for nineteen years. Consequently, many Haitians feared the presence of US troops, worrying that this was just the start of another US occupation. The United States maintained, nonetheless, that its actions were strictly humanitarian in nature, and that the takeover of Haiti's main airport was to ensure that all relief aid intended for the population was safeguarded from looting.

Nearly one month after the earthquake, in early February, yet another problem emerged when ten Baptist missionaries from Idaho were arrested for attempting to take children they claimed were orphans over the Dominican Republic border without proper documentation. The missionaries intended to have the children adopted by US couples. The missionaries pleaded that they were trying to rescue the children from the damage and mayhem of the earthquake, with the promise of a better life in the United States. Haitian officials, however, arrested the missionaries on charges of child trafficking and kidnapping. As it turned out, the children were not all orphans, and although the Americans were eventually freed, many Haitians still believed that they were attempting to steal Haitian children away from their families for the benefit of childless US couples.

Meanwhile, families still searched frantically for missing relatives. The International Red Cross, among other humanitarian actions, set up a website to help reconnect families. The search for survivors continued throughout January, and although the search and rescue mission was officially called off by the Haitian government in late January, people continued to look for their loved ones in the rubble. The last survivor of the quake was discovered on February 8, severely dehydrated, but still alive after being trapped for three weeks.

The Haitian government announced in January the estimated death and injury count for the earthquake: 316,000 killed and at least 300,000 injured. By June 2010, however, the United States Agency for International Development released figures that were far lower than those used by the Haitian government, with an estimated 46,000 to 85,000 dead. The discrepancy caused a controversy among relief agencies: the higher death and injury tolls were better for fundraising. On the other hand, the discrepancy in the figures made potential donors skeptical and wary of giving.

In the earthquake's aftermath, a number of problems have continued. Perhaps most pressing is the violence that plagues women forced to live in the relocation camps because of the loss of their homes. The *New York Times* reported on April 4, 2011:

> Life after Haiti's earthquake has been especially difficult and dangerous for displaced women and girls. In addition to the ongoing crises of homelessness and cholera, a chronic emergency of sexual violence prevails in the settlements where hundreds of thousands still live, well over a year after the disaster.

Likewise, although poverty and disease were constant concerns in the years before the earthquake, in the months and years after the quake, the problems were exacerbated. According to a 2012 study by Tulane University researchers, "More than a third of households affected by the deadly 2010 Haiti earthquake and over half of those living in the camps have not recovered basic household assets nearly two years after the disaster."

The Haiti earthquake resulted in one of the largest multi-nation relief campaigns in history, and yet as of 2012, Haitians remained in dire straits, according to

Ky Luu, executive director of the Disaster Resilience Leadership Academy at Tulane University:

> Despite more than $4 billion in much-needed relief and recovery aid, those living in directly affected areas, especially in camps, are engaging in damaging and unsustainable coping strategies such as reducing food intake. Many who were not part of Haiti's chronically poor before the earthquake are now at risk of becoming so.

To make matters worse, international aid decreased dramatically in the years after the quake, although the recovery was far from over. Nonetheless, there was some hope that a decentralization scheme wherein displaced residents of Port-au-Prince were relocated to the countryside to begin life in cooperative farms might prove helpful to the country as a whole. The United Nations Food and Agriculture Organization "believes that, with enough training and support, about a tenth of the 600,000 people still in earthquake camps could ultimately move to the countryside," according to Randal C. Archibold writing in the *New York Times* on December 25, 2011. If schemes such as these are successful, they may help alleviate Haiti's chronic food shortages and provide jobs for many displaced workers.

Yet Haiti's future seems potentially grim. Although Haiti is slowly emerging from the disaster, it is unlikely the January 2010 earthquake will be its last. In a January 12, 2011, *Christian Science Monitor* article, journalist Pete Spotts reports that geophysicists around the United States believe that there is a great risk of continued slippage on the fault line that resulted in the 2010 quake. Moreover, it is certain that Haiti will continue to be battered by Atlantic and Caribbean hurricanes. Diseases such as cholera continue to ravage the population. The attention given to the Haiti earthquake highlights the ongoing problems besetting the residents of this tiny nation.

World Map

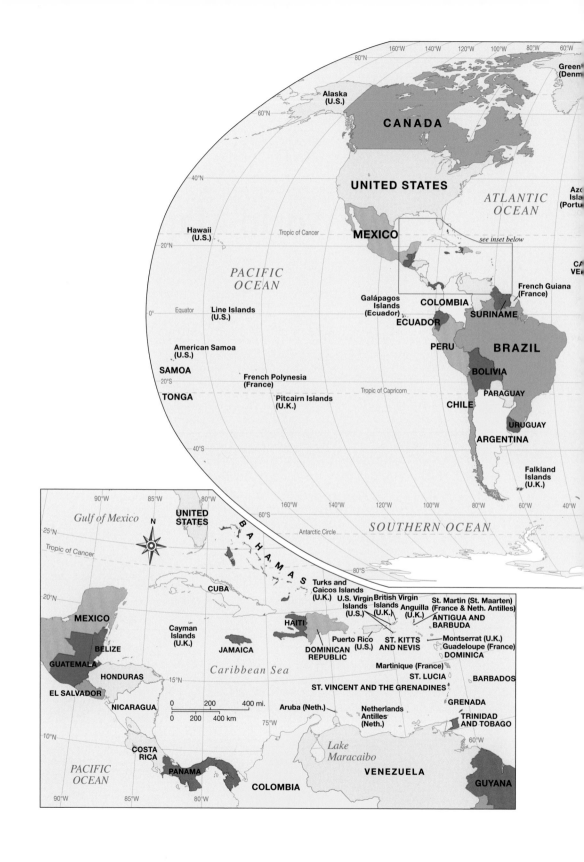

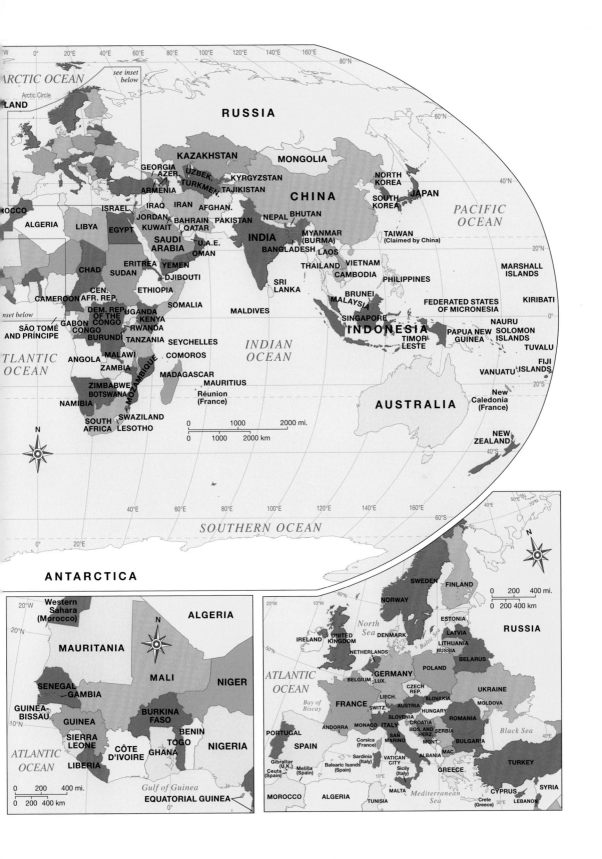

ARCTIC OCEAN

Arctic Circle

see inset below

RUSSIA

KAZAKHSTAN

MONGOLIA

GEORGIA
AZER.
UZBEK.
TURKMEN.
KYRGYZSTAN
ARMENIA
TAJIKISTAN

NORTH KOREA

SOUTH KOREA

JAPAN

CHINA

PACIFIC OCEAN

ISRAEL
IRAQ
IRAN
AFGHAN.

ROCCO

ALGERIA

LIBYA

EGYPT

JORDAN
KUWAIT
BAHRAIN
QATAR
PAKISTAN

NEPAL
BHUTAN

SAUDI ARABIA

U.A.E.
OMAN

INDIA

MYANMAR (BURMA)

TAIWAN (Claimed by China)

BANGLADESH
LAOS

MARSHALL ISLANDS

CHAD
SUDAN

ERITREA
YEMEN

DJIBOUTI

THAILAND

VIETNAM
CAMBODIA

PHILIPPINES

CAMEROON

CEN. AFR. REP.

ETHIOPIA

SRI LANKA

BRUNEI
MALAYSIA

FEDERATED STATES OF MICRONESIA

KIRIBATI

SOMALIA

MALDIVES

SINGAPORE

nset below

SÃO TOMÉ AND PRÍNCIPE

GABON
CONGO

DEM. REP. OF THE CONGO

UGANDA
KENYA

RWANDA

INDONESIA

PAPUA NEW GUINEA

NAURU
SOLOMON ISLANDS

TIMOR-LESTE

TUVALU

BURUNDI

TANZANIA

SEYCHELLES

INDIAN OCEAN

VANUATU

FIJI ISLANDS

TLANTIC OCEAN

ANGOLA

MALAWI

ZAMBIA

MOZAMBIQUE

COMOROS

MADAGASCAR

MAURITIUS

New Caledonia (France)

ZIMBABWE
BOTSWANA

NAMIBIA

Réunion (France)

AUSTRALIA

SOUTH AFRICA

SWAZILAND
LESOTHO

0   1000   2000 mi.

0   1000   2000 km

NEW ZEALAND

N

SOUTHERN OCEAN

ANTARCTICA

Western Sahara (Morocco)

ALGERIA

MAURITANIA

N

MALI

NIGER

SWEDEN
FINLAND

NORWAY

North Sea

ESTONIA

RUSSIA

IRELAND
UNITED KINGDOM
DENMARK

LATVIA

LITHUANIA

RUSSIA

0   200   400 mi.

0   200 400 km

SENEGAL
GAMBIA

GUINEA-BISSAU

GUINEA

BURKINA FASO

BENIN

NETHERLANDS

BELARUS

GERMANY

POLAND

ATLANTIC OCEAN

BELGIUM
LUX.

CZECH REP.

UKRAINE

SIERRA LEONE

TOGO

NIGERIA

Bay of Biscay

LIECH.

FRANCE
SWITZ.

AUSTRIA

SLOVAKIA

HUNGARY

MOLDOVA

CÔTE D'IVOIRE
GHANA

SLOVENIA
CROATIA

ROMANIA

LIBERIA

PORTUGAL

ANDORRA

MONACO
ITALY

SAN MARINO

BOS. AND HERZ.
MONT.

SERBIA

BULGARIA

Black Sea

ATLANTIC OCEAN

SPAIN

Corsica (France)

VATICAN CITY

ALBANIA
MAC.

Gulf of Guinea

EQUATORIAL GUINEA

Gibraltar (U.K.)
Ceuta (Spain)

Melilla (Spain)

Balearic Isands (Spain)

Sardinia (Italy)

Sicily (Italy)

GREECE

TURKEY

0   200   400 mi.

0   200 400 km

MOROCCO

ALGERIA

TUNISIA

MALTA

Crete (Greece)

Mediterranean Sea

CYPRUS
SYRIA

LEBANON

CHAPTER 1

Historical Background on the Haiti Earthquake

Haiti Is Hit by an Earthquake

Gale Student Resources in Context

In the following viewpoint, the writers of *Gale Student Resources in Context* provide an overview of the 7.0 magnitude earthquake that hit Haiti on January 12, 2010. Haiti was vulnerable to natural disasters, and was a very poor country. The earthquake killed thousands of people and displaced more than one million others; the initial tremor and numerous aftershocks caused widespread damage and destruction to homes and businesses. In addition, the quake destroyed most infrastructures, which made it difficult to get aid to those who needed it.

Photo on previous page: Haitians gather to receive bags of rice as food aid in front of the National Palace two weeks after the earthquake. The official residence of the president sustained major damage. (© **Chris Hondros/Getty Images.**)

O n Tuesday, January 12, 2010, at 4:53 P.M. local time, a magnitude 7.0 earthquake struck the Caribbean nation of Haiti. The earthquake was centered approximately 25 kilometers west-southwest of Port-au-Prince, at a depth of approximately 13 kilometers. The United States Geological Survey (USGS) National

---

SOURCE. Gale, *Gale Student Resources in Context.* © 2011 Cengage Learning.

Earthquake Information Center (NEIC) recorded 59 after-shocks of magnitude 4.5 or greater in the 43 days following the initial tremor. The earthquake was felt as far away as The Bahamas, Puerto Rico, southern Florida, northern Columbia, and Northern Venezuela.

Official government estimates include over 225,000 people killed as a direct result of the quake, 300,000 injured, and almost 1.5 million left homeless. Port-au-Prince and other settlements in the region, including Jacmel, Petit-Goâve, and Léogâne, suffered widespread damage and destruction. The majority of residential and commercial buildings, air and sea port facilities, as well as communication and transportation networks were severely impacted. Many of the nation's schools, universities, museums, and churches were also damaged or destroyed.

> The majority of residential and commercial buildings . . . as well as communication and transportation networks were severely impacted.

Haiti's Geography and History

Haiti, along with its neighbor to the east, the Dominican Republic, occupies the island of Hispaniola, located in the Caribbean Sea. Originally inhabited by native Taíno Amerindians, Spanish settlers took over the island following its discovery by Columbus in 1492. In 1697, Spain ceded control of the western third of the island to the French, who built Haiti into one of the wealthiest nations in the Caribbean, relying heavily on slave labor imported from Africa. Toward the end of the 18th century, however, half a million slaves revolted, thus gaining their independence and making Haiti the first black republic in 1804.

Following decades of political violence and corruption, the nation of Haiti remains one of the poorest nations in the world, and among the most vulnerable to natural disasters. Hurricanes are a common threat to the tiny nation. Rains brought by these storms cause widespread flooding; the vast majority of Haiti's forests

Haiti's Housing Situation Prior to the Earthquake

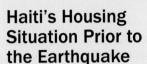

Before the earthquake, the city and metropolitan area of Port-au-Prince, as well as most towns in the countryside, were characterized by uncontrolled urbanization. The hills surrounding these towns and cities are covered with dwellings of variable quality. A study carried out in 1997 showed that 67% of the urban population lived in spontaneous settlements that covered only 22% of inhabited land. Half of the slums are located on steep slopes or at the bottom of gullies; the houses are in danger of being swept away by torrents during periods of heavy rain or hurricanes. Inner-city and coastal slums are also exposed to floods as they are located close to catchment areas. Soil erosion is therefore a serious problem for the housing sector. The absence of earthquake-resistant materials in construction and the total lack of control over development increase the vulnerability of this sector.

Uncontrolled urbanization also makes it difficult to provide services such as water, energy, sanitation, and household waste collection. The majority of slums have no road system. Steep slopes make it very difficult to build access roads, and most roads, if there are any, are not paved and must be repaired after each rainy season.

Housing in poor neighborhoods, which can have up to three stories, is usually built with post and beam structures with an infill of perpend and concrete slabs. The advantage of this type of construction, especially concrete slabs, is the use of hurricane-resistant materials. But the under-proportioning of structures (particularly [the] subsequent addition of a storey), defective reinforcement, and poor quality concrete with an insignificant proportion of cement make these buildings particularly dangerous in seismic zones.

SOURCE. Haiti Earthquake PDNA: Assessment of Damage, Losses, General and Sectoral Needs, *March 2010, p. 73.*

have been harvested for fuel, leaving its mostly mountainous terrain vulnerable to erosion and mudslides. In a country as poor as this, there are few resources to cope with natural disasters. Disease and starvation continue to

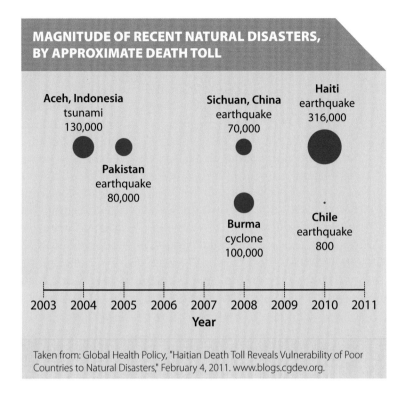

MAGNITUDE OF RECENT NATURAL DISASTERS, BY APPROXIMATE DEATH TOLL

Aceh, Indonesia tsunami 130,000

Pakistan earthquake 80,000

Sichuan, China earthquake 70,000

Burma cyclone 100,000

Haiti earthquake 316,000

Chile earthquake 800

2003 2004 2005 2006 2007 2008 2009 2010 2011
Year

Taken from: Global Health Policy, "Haitian Death Toll Reveals Vulnerability of Poor Countries to Natural Disasters," February 4, 2011. www.blogs.cgdev.org.

claim lives long after the initial devastation has occurred. Between 2004 and 2008, hurricanes accounted for more than four thousand deaths and left millions homeless or dislocated. Lack of potable water, food and waterborne diseases, and more recently, the spread of AIDS represent ongoing threats to the population of Haiti.

Seismic Conditions

Running through the southern peninsula of Haiti lies the Enriquillo-Plaintain Garden fault, an east-west strike-slip fault, and one of several fault zones that surround the Gonâve Microplate, which separates the North American Plate and the Caribbean Plate. (The earth's crust is made up of several major and minor tectonic plates, the motion of which is driven by heat from the earth's mantle.) Scientists have determined that the January 12th quake was caused by a rupture in the Enriquillo fault, within the boundaries of the Caribbean and North American plates. Other major quakes have been associated with this fault system—two of them, in 1751 and 1770, destroyed the capital city; the last major quake to hit the region occurred in 1860.

Extensive Damage

The USGS PAGER[1] summary for the Haiti region on January 12th estimated that over 2.3 million people had been exposed to violent tremor activity. Structural damage was also predicted to be very heavy in cities and villages close the quake's origin. Most of the buildings in and around Port-au-Prince, as well as in some rural areas, were constructed of concrete masonry or block. Similar materials were used in floors and roofs for most multi-story buildings. Observers from the USGS Earthquake Engineering Research Institute (EERI) observed that most of the residential and commercial buildings damaged during the quake were concrete structures, many without adequate reinforcements needed to resist the seismic forces dealt by the earthquake. The weight of these structures also appeared to be a factor; most of the intact buildings left behind were of lighter wood or metal construction.

As is often the case during a severe earthquake, most of the casualties were the result of people being crushed or trapped inside buildings that collapsed in the moments following the first tremors. The bulk of the casualties were Haitian citizens, but there were a significant number of foreign embassy and United Nations staff, aid workers, and tourists among the casualties. As many as 200 guests at the famous Hotel Montana, in Port-au-Prince, were killed or presumed dead; the collapse of the Presidential Palace resulted in the loss of several high ranking government officials. The nation's communications and transportation infrastructure was severely damaged. Cell phone coverage was all but knocked out, roads were impassible, harbor and marine port facilities destroyed, and control of the only major airport in the region had to be handed over to controllers from the United States, who were better able to manage air traffic into and out of the facility.

> "Medical facilities, or what was left of them, were quickly overwhelmend with injured and dying patients."

Aftermath and Response

In the first hours following the quake, medical facilities, or what was left of them, were quickly overwhelmed with injured and dying patients. The morgue in Port-au-Prince was filled, and thousands of bodies were left lining the city's streets. Tens of thousands remained trapped, injured and dying, under the rubble. Those who survived slept on the streets and in makeshift camps, afraid to re-enter their homes for fear they would eventually collapse.

Military units and humanitarian agencies were among the first to provide support and relief. Médecins Sans Frontières (Doctors Without Borders) quickly set up operations in two of the capital city's damaged hospitals; International Red Cross also began to fly in food and water, as well as trained specialists in search and rescue, disaster response, and family services. Members of the U.S. Army's 82nd Airborne were quickly deployed to the island to help distribute food and assist other aid organizations with their missions. Just over a week following the quake, the U.S. Navy's hospital ship USNS *Comfort* arrived in Port-au-Prince Harbor to serve as a field hospital for quake victims.

In the weeks following the disaster, both government and non-government organizations had raised hundreds of millions of dollars to finance relief efforts in Haiti. Roughly half the money raised would go to buy food, water, and other relief supplies. Organizations such as the American Red Cross and the United States Agency for International Development (USAID) would

also focus their efforts on providing labor and materials needed to construct shelter for the nearly one-million left homeless and living in refugee camps around the city.

By early April, countries around the world, working through the United Nations, had pledged nearly 10 billion dollars in both short and long term aid to Haiti. According to the U.N., damage and losses caused by the January 12 earthquake would exceed 7 billion. It is hoped that the moneys raised will be used to reconstruct the nation's infrastructure, including schools, hospitals, and government facilities.

The poor neighborhood of Canape Vert lies in ruins following the January 2010 earthquake in Port-au-Prince, Haiti. (© **Frederic Dupoux/Getty Images.**)

Note

1. While seismic data reflects the nature and extent of ground movement during an earthquake, it does little to assess the potential impact such an event has on the population within the affected area. For this, the USGS created the PAGER system, which helps predict the number of people exposed to earthquake activity, and incorporates the Modified Mercalli Intensity Scale, a set of intensity values, ranging from I to X (1 to 10), based on the observed structural damage resulting from an earthquake. The system is intended to inform emergency response teams, government officials, and the media as to the severity and scope of a potential disaster caused by earthquakes around the world.

The Red Cross Rushes to Get Supplies to Survivors of the Haiti Earthquake

International Committee of the Red Cross

In the following viewpoint, the International Committee of the Red Cross (ICRC) describes the situation in Haiti immediately after the earthquake and their response. The ICRC rushed food, water, and medical aid to the stricken nation; however, the collapse of infrastructure created serious challenges to the ICRC in delivering the aid where it was needed. Nevertheless, within days of the quake, the Red Cross established medical facilities, water stations, and telecommunication linkages. In addition, the ICRC set up a system whereby families separated by the quake could reconnect with each other. The ICRC is an international emergency response aid agency.

Significant amounts of emergency aid have arrived in quake-struck Port-au-Prince. The challenge now is to get it to survivors as quickly as possible. Further assessments confirm that the damage is widespread and immense. Very few neighbourhoods have been spared, while local infrastructure and services have been wiped out. The ICRC [International Committee of the Red Cross] has built latrines for 1,000 people and supplied medical kits for 2,000 patients to two hospitals. Seven truckloads of ICRC medical supplies should arrive in the capital on Sunday evening.

Supplies Are Desperately Needed

Tens of thousands of quake survivors have spent a fifth night outdoors in the makeshift camps that have sprung up in every neighbourhood in Port-au-Prince. Access to shelter, toilets, water, food and medical care remains extremely limited, according to ICRC specialists on the ground. While some food seems to be available in the city, prices have skyrocketed and most people cannot afford to buy anything.

Medical facilities in Port-au-Prince still lack staff and medicine. They are overwhelmed and bursting at the seams. The sanitation situation in the makeshift camps is precarious.

"Croix de Pré may be the most devastated neighbourhood in Port-au-Prince," says ICRC spokesman, Simon Schorno, who has visited most areas of [the] city. "Very few buildings are left standing and in every back alley, people have pitched their plastic sheets and blankets. Some survivors sit in smashed and dusty cars. There is trash everywhere and the air is filled with the stench of dead bodies," he says.

> " Red Cross volunteers . . . clean and stitch up wounds amidst the rubble. "

The ICRC, which was already present and active in Haiti before Tuesday's earthquake, is strengthening its

Haitians wait in line for food aid at a downtown Port-au-Prince distribution point in January 2010, as aftershocks continue to rock the Haitian capital, complicating relief efforts. (© Carol Guzy/Washington Post/Getty Images.)

response to the crisis. It works as part of the wider International Red Cross and Red Crescent Movement and cooperates closely with the Haitian Red Cross.

According to Mr. Schorno, the headquarters of the Haitian Red Cross, which is located near Croix de Pré, is surrounded by people looking for medical care. The National Society has set up a first aid post in the middle of the street, where Red Cross volunteers from Haiti and other countries work side-by-side to clean and stitch up wounds amidst the rubble.

Death and Desperation

In Centreville, on the Place du Champ de Mars, several thousand survivors are now living in one of the city's largest makeshift camps. Mr. Schorno describes a desperate situation there. "Some people have found a bit of shade but most sit in the sun. The stench of stale urine is overpowering. Hundreds of children improvise games, laugh and cry. Mothers chat with neighbours and fan themselves," he says.

Martine, a 39-year-old mother, washes her son in a bucket of water. Several families have already used it. Her husband left earlier in the morning to fetch drinking water. For now, they have none. Her neighbours gave her a few vegetables they had cooked. "I don't know how long we'll stay or where we'll go," she says.

The streets further towards the sea are packed with people. Aftershocks continue and no one wants to be inside the few buildings left standing.

"There are bloated, decomposing bodies in the streets, many leaking yellow liquid," says Mr. Schorno. "Motorcycles and cars drive around them, and no one looks. Young men remove blocks of cement from collapsed buildings. They are not looking for people, but for scrap metal. It seems they are now focused only on their own survival."

Racing to Save Lives

In the shadow of the flattened National Palace, the police headquarters is empty and the building half-collapsed. Police officers and their families, who are also in need of help, sit in their cars and pickup trucks. Rémi, the three-year-old son of one officer, is sick and injured.

"He was under the building for four hours and has been paralysed since we moved him out of the rubble, three days ago," says his father. "I am scared," whispers his mother, Wilma. "Is my boy going to die?" Her son, who has not eaten in two days and is unresponsive, is taken to a nearby field hospital. It is the only functioning medical facility in Montrissant. There are four doctors for around 400 patients waiting at the makeshift clinic, which is made up of two metal containers and [a] canvas-covered courtyard.

It is packed and there are dozens of wounded and sick people at the gate. "One of the doctors told me they cannot cope and lost over 50 patients in the past two days," says Mr. Schorno. Around 50 expatriate doctors are expected to arrive soon, but for some survivors, like Rémi, the help may be too late.

> Everyone you talk to has lost someone.

"Closer to the sea, huge piles of black and white trash are piling up, grey polluted water floods the streets, ladies sell dirty vegetables, and young men are cutting up used car tires," says Mr. Schorno. "Buses blowing clouds of black smoke are full. Those who can are leaving the city for the countryside, where it might be easier to survive and perhaps start anew."

No One Is Left Untouched

Before the quake, the Haitian Red Cross had around 1,000 registered volunteers in Port-au-Prince, many of whom have since been working around-the-clock to help those in need.

"We have saved many lives in the last few days," says Judas Celoge, the field coordinator for the Haitian Red Cross's first aid post in Martissant—one of the poorest neighbourhoods in the city.

Near the first aid table on the side of the street, 13-year-old Marine sits on the sidewalk holding her head in her hands. She doesn't cry but stares emptily ahead. She lost both her parents and her brother and sister in the quake. Their bodies have not been found and probably never will be.

"Everyone you talk to has lost someone. There is no one here that has not been affected by this tragedy," says Mr. Schorno.

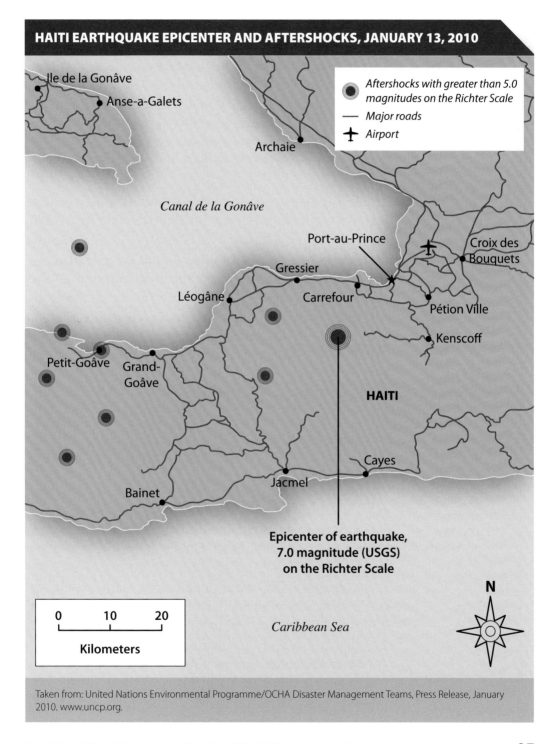

HAITI EARTHQUAKE EPICENTER AND AFTERSHOCKS, JANUARY 13, 2010

Ile de la Gonâve

Anse-a-Galets

Archaie

Aftershocks with greater than 5.0
magnitudes on the Richter Scale

— Major roads

✈ Airport

Canal de la Gonâve

Port-au-Prince

Croix des Bouquets

Gressier

Léogâne

Carrefour

Pétion Ville

Kenscoff

Petit-Goâve

Grand-Goâve

HAITI

Cayes

Jacmel

Bainet

Epicenter of earthquake,
7.0 magnitude (USGS)
on the Richter Scale

0   10   20

Kilometers

Caribbean Sea

N

Taken from: United Nations Environmental Programme/OCHA Disaster Management Teams, Press Release, January 2010. www.uncp.org.

The ICRC Provides Water and Medical Supplies

The international relief activities of the Red Cross and Red Crescent, including those of the ICRC, are being coordinated by the International Federation of Red Cross and Red Crescent Societies (IFRC).

The ICRC continues to work closely with its Red Cross partners on the ground to assess humanitarian needs and deliver relief assistance.

A shipment of around 40 tonnes of ICRC medical supplies, sent from Geneva on Thursday night, is finally expected to arrive in Port-au-Prince on Sunday evening. It will arrive by truck from the Dominican Republic.

On Saturday, 16 January, the ICRC started a water trucking programme in the Delmas neighbourhood, which is now providing clean water for around 1,000 people living in a makeshift camp. Latrines have also been built in the same neighbourhood.

> The ICRC is not in a position to provide exact figures about the number of deaths or injuries.

The ICRC, with the support of the Haitian Red Cross, has supplied medical kits to treat 2,000 patients for a month to two Port-au-Prince referral hospitals. Hundreds of blankets and plastic sheets have also been distributed.

Given the scope of the disaster, the ICRC is not in a position to provide exact figures about the number of deaths or injuries resulting from the earthquake.

A second ICRC rapid deployment team left Geneva on Sunday morning for Haiti, where they will provide additional forensics, tracing, nursing, communications and logistics support to staff already on the ground.

Meanwhile, the first of three massive Red Cross Red Crescent basic health care emergency response units (ERUs) arrived on 16 January. The ERU is designed to provide basic and immediate health care to 30,000 people. So far, 14 ERUs have been deployed to Haiti, with most expected to arrive in the coming days. They include water and sanitation units, logistic units, IT and telecommunication infrastructure, and a massive 250-bed hospital.

In addition, ICRC Delegates have visited several places of detention in Port-au-Prince to assess the needs of the detainees and the authorities, and to follow up on detention issues.

The ICRC Helps Families Reconnect

The ICRC is working to set up a post at the headquarters of the Haitian Red Cross to help restore family links between people who may have been separated or who are searching for missing relatives. People will also be able to register as safe and well. The post will ensure that people can receive and forward information to their relatives.

As of 17 January, more than 21,600 people had registered with the ICRC's special website, www.icrc.org/familylinks, which was activated on Thursday to help people searching for their loved ones.

The overwhelming majority of registrations are from people looking for news about their relatives, although around 1,500 people have so far used the site to say they were safe and alive.

"The large number of people who have registered the names of their loved ones is a clear indicator of how many people outside Haiti are really desperate for news," says Robert Zimmerman, who's in charge of the ICRC's Restoring Family Links programme.

"It's going to take some time, though, before we're able to collect significant amounts of information from within Haiti. We're trying to get the word out that this service exists and that people can let the Red Cross know they're okay, but for the anxious relatives waiting for news, it's going to require patience and time."

US President Barack Obama Outlines Relief Efforts in Haiti

Barack Obama

In the following viewpoint, US president Barack Obama responds to the devastation of the Haiti earthquake, reporting that US rescue and relief workers have arrived in Haiti to help with the disaster recovery. The US military has arrived in Haiti and secured the airport. President Obama notes that US citizens in Haiti are his highest priority and that many have already been airlifted out of the country. In addition, he pledges the full help and cooperation of the United States for all the peoples of Haiti as they work to recover from the earthquake.

I've directed my administration to launch a swift, coordinated and aggressive effort to save lives and support the recovery in Haiti.

SOURCE. Barack Obama, "Remarks by the President on Recovery Efforts in Haiti," White House, January 14, 2010. whitehouse .gov. Copyright © 2010 by the White House. All rights reserved. Reproduced by permission.

Haiti Suffers Devastating Losses

The losses that have been suffered in Haiti are nothing less than devastating, and responding to a disaster of this magnitude will require every element of our national capacity—our diplomacy and development assistance; the power of our military; and, most importantly, the compassion of our country. And this morning, I'm joined by several members of my national security team who are leading this coordinated response.

I've made it clear to each of these leaders that Haiti must be a top priority for their departments and agencies right now. This is one of those moments that calls out for American leadership. For the sake of our citizens who are in Haiti, for the sake of the Haitian people who have suffered so much, and for the sake of our common humanity, we stand in solidarity with our neighbors to the south, knowing that but for the grace of God, there we go.

This morning, I can report that the first waves of our rescue and relief workers are on the ground and at work. A survey team worked overnight to identify priority areas for assistance, and shared the results of that review throughout the United States government, and with international partners who are also sending support. Search and rescue teams are actively working to save lives. Our military has secured the airport and prepared it to receive the heavy equipment and resources that are on the way, and to receive them around the clock, 24 hours a day. An airlift has been set up to deliver high-priority items like water and medicine. And we're coordinating closely with the Haitian government, the United Nations, and other countries who are also on the ground.

We have no higher priority than the safety of American citizens, and we've airlifted injured Americans out of Haiti. We're running additional evacuations, and will continue to do so in the days ahead. I know that many Americans, especially Haitian Americans, are desperate for information about their family and friends. And the State Department has set up a phone number and e-mail address . . . to inquire about your loved ones. And you should know that we will not rest until we account for our fellow Americans in harm's way.

Even as we move as quickly as possible, it will take hours—and in many cases days—to get all of our people and resources on the ground. Right now in Haiti roads are impassable, the main port is badly damaged, communications are just beginning to come online, and aftershocks continue.

US Relief Efforts Are on the Way

None of this will seem quick enough if you have a loved one who's trapped, if you're sleeping on the streets, if you can't feed your children. But it's important that everybody in Haiti understand, at this very moment one of the largest relief efforts in our recent history is moving towards Haiti. More American search and rescue teams are coming. More food. More water. Doctors, nurses, paramedics. More of the people, equipment and capabilities that can make the difference between life and death.

The United States armed forces are also on their way to support this effort. Several Coast Guard cutters are already there providing everything from basic services like water, to vital technical support for this massive logistical operation. Elements of the Army's 82nd Airborne Division will arrive today. We're also deploying a Marine Expeditionary Unit, the aircraft carrier USS Carl Vinson, and the Navy's hospital ship, the Comfort.

And today, I'm also announcing an immediate investment of $100 million to support our relief efforts. This will mean more of the life-saving equipment, food, water and medicine that will be needed. This investment will grow over the coming year as we embark on the long-term recovery from this unimaginable tragedy.

US president Barack Obama (foreground) met with Haitian president René Préval in Washington, DC, in March 2010 to discuss relief efforts. (© **AP Images/ Pablo Martinez Monsivais.**)

The United States Will Partner with Haiti

The United States of America will also forge the partnerships that this undertaking demands. We will partner with the Haitian people. And that includes the government of Haiti, which needs our support as they recover from the devastation of this earthquake. It also includes the many Haitian Americans who are determined to help their friends and family. And I've asked Vice President [Joe] Biden to meet in South Florida this weekend with members of the Haitian American community, and with responders who are mobilizing to help the Haitian people.

We will partner with the United Nations and its dedicated personnel and peacekeepers, especially those from Brazil, who are already on the ground due to their outstanding peacekeeping efforts there. And I want to say that our hearts go out to the United Nations, which has experienced one of the greatest losses in its history. We have no doubt that we can carry on the work that was done by so many of the U.N. effort that have been lost, and we see that their legacy is Haiti's hope for the future.

We will partner with other nations and organizations. And that's why I've been reaching out to leaders from across the Americas and beyond who are sending resources to support this effort. And we will join with the strong network of non-governmental organizations across the country who understand the daily struggles of the Haitian people.

A Call for Generosity and Compassion

Yet even as we bring our resources to bear on this emergency, we need to summon the tremendous generosity and compassion of the American people. I want to thank the many Americans who have already contributed to this effort. I want to encourage all Americans who want to help to go to whitehouse.gov to learn more. And in the days ahead, we will continue to work with those individuals and organizations who want to assist this effort so that you can do so.

Finally, I want to speak directly to the people of Haiti. Few in the world have endured the hardships that you have known. Long before this tragedy, daily life itself was often a bitter struggle. And after suffering so much for so long, to face this new horror must cause some to look up and ask, have we somehow been forsaken?

> You will not be forsaken; you will not be forgotten. . . . America stands with you.

To the people of Haiti, we say clearly, and with conviction, you will not be forsaken; you will not be forgotten. In this, your hour of greatest need, America stands with you. The world stands with you. We know that you are a strong and resilient people. You have endured a history of slavery and struggle, of natural disaster and recovery. And through it all, your spirit has been unbroken and your faith has been unwavering. So today, you must know that help is arriving—much, much more help is on the way.

Canada Responds Swiftly to the Haiti Earthquake

John Geddes

Canadian journalist John Geddes reports on the establishment of the Stabilization and Reconstruction Task Force (START), which is a secretariat created by the Foreign Affairs Department of the Canadian government. The mission of START is to provide a quick and efficient response to disasters worldwide. START is credited with Canada's swift response to the Haiti earthquake and for bringing much needed supplies, shelter, and humanitarian relief to Haiti. Canada has close ties to Haiti because there are many Haitian immigrants living in Quebec. Geddes writes on politics and policy for *Maclean's* magazine.

The pattern in Ottawa following a humanitarian crisis has long been predictable: first the scramble to help, then the political damage-control exercise to justify delays and disarray. After the Indian Ocean tsunami in 2004, federal officials were left explaining why

SOURCE. John Geddes, "Yes, We Have a Plan: Canada's Speedy Response to the Haiti Crisis Was No Accident," *Maclean's*, vol. 123, February 15, 2010, p. 18. Copyright © 2010 by Maclean's. All rights reserved. Reproduced by permission.

it took several precious days to lease a Russian aircraft to fly in a Canadian military disaster relief team. When Israel attacked Hezbollah fighters in Lebanon in 2006, other countries managed to begin evacuating their citizens while Canadian officials were trying to book ships to do the job.

> Experts in large-scale relief operations have generally applauded the Canadian effort.

But last month's devastating earthquake in Haiti has been an entirely different story. Although some inevitable snags have been reported, experts in large-scale relief operations have generally applauded the Canadian effort. "We can see," said Susan Johnson, director general of international operations for the Canadian Red Cross, "that we're in a different place than we were in some previous responses on the part of Canada." Prime Minister Stephen Harper and his cabinet are basking in the praise—a welcome distraction from sharp and sustained criticism of the decision to suspend Parliament until after the Winter Olympics.

The more agile reaction this time is no accident. The federal government's capacity to coordinate operations after a major disaster abroad has been systematically overhauled in recent years, precisely because it was previously found wanting. Among the old shortcomings: no large central stockpile of emergency aid supplies, no single federal agency with the authority to pull together the response, not even a full roster of trained public servants to call in to man the phones in an operations room.

The Role of the Stabilization and Reconstruction Task Force

The focal point of the updated system is a new secretariat in the Foreign Affairs Department called START, for Stabilization and Reconstruction Task Force. Invisible to the public, START is largely responsible for orchestrating the Haitian earthquake response, and the task force is

Help for Haiti from Around the World

The Haiti relief effort was an international affair. Some notable examples:

- China donated US $1 million to Haiti relief.
- Cuba maintained emergency field hospitals.
- The European Council pledged €429 million (US $600 million) in emergency, humanitarian, and reconstruction aid.
- Digicel, an Irish telecommunications company, pledged to repair the damaged telephone network.
- Mexico sent doctors, search-and-rescue dogs, and medical equipment.
- Sweden sent water purification equipment, medical aid, tents, and financial aid.
- The United Kingdom sent firefighters with search-and-rescue dogs and equipment.
- The United Nations sent US $10 million in emergency funds.
- The United States sent ships, helicopters, planes, and Marines.

expected to play the key role in managing the transition from a humanitarian-relief sprint to a reconstruction marathon.

START's core role is to make sure the federal government's sometimes fractious parts—especially Foreign Affairs, the Canadian International Development Agency [CIDA] and the Department of National Defence—mesh in a crisis. "It's sometimes considered trite when people talk about a 'whole-of-government' approach," Peter Kent, the federal minister of state responsible for the

Americas, told *Maclean's*. "But START has really brought together the departmental leadership, the professionals, and the political leadership right up to the Prime Minister."

Although it was created in 2005, the year after the South Asian tsunami, START really began to take shape in 2006. After some growing pains, it was extensively reorganized beginning last spring. That was when Elissa Golberg was appointed to head the task force, after attracting favourable media and political attention during a stint in Afghanistan serving in the sensitive post of representative of Canada in Kandahar. Outside groups working closely with the federal government in Haiti regard Golberg as a linchpin. "I think her skills and experience are shining through at a time like this, her ability to pull people together and coordinate," said Johnson.

As it happened, Golberg was not in Ottawa when the earthquake struck. She was in Beijing, where she had been leading a two-day disaster training session at the Canadian embassy, and had to rush home. So the U.S. Geological Survey email alert signalling that Haiti had been rocked by an earthquake on the evening of Jan. 12 flashed onto the screens of her staff while she was away. Within a few hours START had convened the standing interdepartmental task force that takes charge of the federal response to an overseas disaster. That group—co-chaired by Golberg and the head of Foreign Affairs' Latin America bureau—has since been meeting daily to coordinate the government's reaction.

New Elements of Canadian Relief Efforts

Many crucial elements in the response are surprisingly new. The most visible are the new C-17s, the behemoth strategic-lift aircraft delivered by Boeing to the Canadian Forces in 2007 and 2008. In fact, the availability of the planes for Haiti was partly good luck—they might well have been in the Middle East hauling supplies in and out of Afghanistan, in which case Canada would have had to lease private aircraft for the Haitian relief effort. Another key new element was a new CIDA stockpile of emergency supplies, built up since 2004, and warehoused in Mississauga, Ont. The field hospital in Haiti—run jointly by the Canadian and Norwegian Red Cross, and funded partly by the Canadian government—only came into existence over the past few years.

Huge planes, pallets mounded with relief supplies, and an emergency hospital were the most visible signs of the Canadian answer to the cry for help. Far less obvious, but crucial, are new arrangements to make sure the right people get deployed quickly. Only in the last eight months, START created a division to oversee one-stop shopping for experts from various branches of the federal government, the provinces and non-governmental groups—from prison workers, to experts on border controls, to justice officials. Also invisible, except to insiders, is the evidently improved working relationship between Harper's cabinet and the bureaucrats since, say, the Lebanon evacuation of 2006. "It is obvious to observers that the civil service and the political leadership understand each other better and co-operate better when faced with a crisis like this," said Scott Gilmore, the Ottawa-based executive director of Peace Dividend Trust, a non-profit group that works with peace and humanitarian missions, including a large operation in Haiti.

Haiti has been by far START's highest-profile test to date, but hardly the task force's first real-world challenge. Considering earthquakes alone, there were devastating ones in Pakistan in 2005, Indonesia in 2006, Peru in 2007, and China in 2008. After each crisis, START conducted post-mortem analyses of what worked and what went wrong. But it's not just a humanitarian-relief unit. It's also responsible for developing federal policy on fragile states, like Haiti, Sudan and Afghanistan, and deliver-

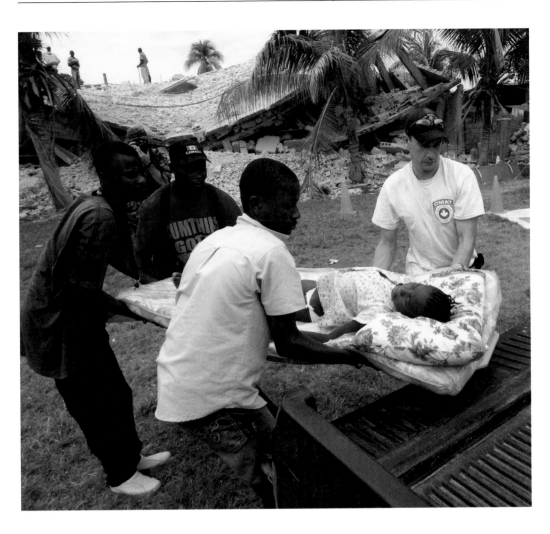

ing programs in those countries aimed at peacekeeping, peacemaking and preventing conflicts from erupting. Even before the earthquake, START was in Haiti working on projects like reforming the country's notorious prisons and shoring up its border with the Dominican Republic.

Canadians Take the Long View

It's the long view of Haiti's future that will matter most as START grapples with how to take the momentum behind the disaster response and convert it into a plan

Canadian doctors load a young woman onto a truck outside a medical clinic in Leogane, Haiti. Canada was among the countries that supplied health care workers to assist in the weeks following the earthquake. (© AP Images/Ryan Remiorz.)

to rebuild the battered country. Johnson points out that unlike Sri Lanka after the 2004 tsunami—when coastal communities were hard hit but the capital, Colombo, was intact—Haiti's capital, Port-au-Prince, lies in ruins. The earthquake "took out the country's nervous system," she said. Reconstruction will mean not only clearing roads and building houses, but restoring institutions that were far from robust even before this latest blow.

> Canada's ties to the desperately poor country, centred around the large Haitian immigrant community in Quebec, are dense.

Haiti is relatively close and Canada's ties to the desperately poor country, centred around the large Haitian immigrant community in Quebec, are dense. Next week the Canadian Red Cross will host a meeting in Montreal of key Red Cross officials from many countries on next steps in Haiti. Nobody expects anything but a long slog, in which the earthquake will come to seem like a punctuation mark in a history of hardship. "These little kids that we see, the survivors coming out of the rubble," Kent said, "they will be adults by the time we actually get to a point of meaningful recovery and reconstruction in Haiti." The question now is whether the new way of operating behind Canada's surprisingly strong start in aiding that recovery will be enough to sustain its momentum.

Violence Flares in Haiti

Lucy Cockcroft

In the following viewpoint, British journalist Lucy Cockcroft reports on the days immediately following the Haiti earthquake, when armed gangs took to the streets to find food and water. Looting and rioting were widespread. Some residents resorted to violence to protect their belongings from looters. The violence made disbursement of much needed supplies difficult, and US troops were called in to provide security.

Chaos and fear reigned on the streets of the capital Port-au-Prince on Sunday, as many were still waiting for food, water and medicine five days after the disaster decimated the area.

Police opened fire on a group of looters, killing at least one of them, as hundreds of rioters ransacked a supermarket.

SOURCE. Lucy Cockcroft, "Haiti Earthquake: 10,000 US Soldiers Due as Violence on Streets Intensifies," *Daily Telegraph* (UK), January 17, 2010. Copyright © 2010 by Telegraph Media Group Limited. All rights reserved. Reproduced by permission.

Haitians loot in the downtown business district. Looting was rampant following the earthquake, as people struggled to find aid and food. (© Niki Kahn/ Washington Post/Getty Images.)

One, a man in his 30s, was killed outright by bullets to the head as the crowd grabbed produce in the Marche Hyppolite [the Iron Market, a large shopping area].

Another quickly snatched the rucksack off the dead man's back as clashes continued and police reinforcements descended on the area armed with pump-action shotguns and assault rifles.

Residents in the Delmas area caught two suspected looters, tied them together, beat them and dragged them through the streets. Both were eventually dumped, motionless.

Roving Gangs Cause Violence

Gangs of men on Boulevard Jean-Jacques Dessalines, their faces covered with bandannas to mask both their identity and the smell of decaying bodies, brandished machetes and sharpened planks of wood as they ran from shop to shop stealing shoes, rolls of carpet and cooking pots.

Despite being outnumbered, officers tried to disperse the violence, shouting at passers-by to leave the area. Elsewhere there were reports of officers stepping aside to allow vigilantes to deal with looters.

"Haitians are partly taking things into their own hands. There are no jails, the criminals are running free, there are no authorities controlling this," said Eddy Toussaint, who witnessed the violence.

It is hoped that armed American troops will quell the unrest when they arrive, but it is unclear exactly when that will be. Canada has also promised to send 1,000 troops to support the relief effort, in addition to the 500 already there.

> Gangs of men . . . brandished machetes and sharpened planks of wood as they ran from shop to shop stealing.

The Relief Effort Is Hampered

Trickles of aid are managing to get through, but much of the relief effort is being hampered by the logistical problems of transporting it from the small and damaged airport and into the town.

Médecins Sans Frontières [Doctors Without Borders] said that a cargo plane carrying an inflatable field hospital with the capacity to hold more than 100 patients was denied permission to land and had to be re-routed through the Dominican Republic, creating a 24-hour delay.

Alain Joyandet, French co-operation minister, protested to Washington about the US military's management of the airport after a French medical aid flight was turned away.

The US Army is working to open a critical port in Haiti to help the flow of aid, and helicopters have been drafted in to distribute supplies.

So far they have delivered over 70,000 bottles of water and 130,000 food rations, "and we're going to be able to increase that every day," Lieutenant General PK Keen, deputy commander of US southern Command, said.

"But, clearly, this is a disaster of epic proportions, and we've got a lot of work ahead of us."

Vast queues formed at distribution points where the UN World Food Programme handed out high-energy food which had been delivered under armed guard.

Florence Louis, 29, seven months pregnant with two children, was one of thousands of Haitians who gathered at a gate at the Cite Soleil slum.

Clutching four packs of biscuits, she said: "It is enough because I didn't have anything at all."

Thirst and Hunger Leads to Violence

On another street in Port-au-Prince, six young men ripped water pipes off walls to suck out the few drops inside.

"This is very, very bad, but I am too thirsty," said Pierre Louis Delmar.

It is also understood that two Dominicans were shot and seriously wounded as they handed out aid.

Carlos Gatas and Milton Matos struggled back to the Dominican Republic embassy with gunshot wounds after the apparent attack.

There were also reports of a crowd of starving Haitians fighting each other with machetes over small packages of food dropped into a stadium by a helicopter.

The UN said increasing numbers of Haitians were trying to cross the border into the Dominican Republic, on the eastern side of Hispaniola island, and reported a surge of quake survivors fleeing to northern cities.

> "Starving Haitians [fought] each other with machetes over small packages of food.

The Most Serious Crisis in Decades

UN Secretary-General Ban Ki-Moon, who visited Haiti yesterday, called the earthquake "one of the most serious crises in decades.

"The damage, destruction and loss of life are just overwhelming," he added.

The United Nations was feeding 40,000 people a day and hoped to increase that to 1 million within two weeks, he said. "The challenge at this time is how to co-ordinate all of this outpouring of assistance."

It is not yet known how many died in Tuesday's 7.0-magnitude earthquake, as, helped by international rescue workers, survivors still emerge from the rubble against the odds and many remain unaccounted for.

Haiti's government alone has already recovered 20,000 bodies—not counting those recovered by independent agencies or relatives themselves, Jean-Max Bellerive, the Prime Minister of Haiti, said.

The Pan American Health Organization now says 50,000 to 100,000 people perished in the quake, although American military sources have suggested it could exceed 200,000.

The Haitian government has also estimated that 1.5 million have been left homeless, and face another night without shelter.

US Troops Arrive in Haiti to Provide Aid and Security

Ed Pilkington

> In the following viewpoint, *Guardian* news correspondent Ed Pilkington covers the arrival of US troops in Haiti following the earthquake. He notes that the troops were uniform in their desire to help the Haitians as opposed to fighting battles. He also reports that moving in so many troops looked unnervingly like an invasion. Despite this, and previous US military interventions, Pilkington concludes, the Haitian people were peaceful and welcomed the arrival of the troops.

The US paratrooper had a simple message for the people of Haiti. Dressed in khaki, carrying an assault rifle and with the iconic sight of Black Hawk helicopters taking off behind him, he said:

SOURCE. Ed Pilkington, "Haiti: We're Not Here to Fight, US Troops Insist," *Guardian*, January 18, 2010. Copyright Guardian News and Media Ltd 2010. Reproduced by permission of the publisher.

"I don't plan on firing a single shot while I'm here. I've been in Iraq three times and I've done enough of that." . . .

US Troops Come as Helpers, Not Warriors

The paratrooper was part of the 82nd airborne division from Fort Bragg, North Carolina, a toughened crew of battle-ready fighters accustomed to forming the front-line in many American war efforts.

This time, though, they and their commanding officers—right up to the rank of commander-in-chief, Barack Obama—were keen as mustard to present themselves as helpers and carers, not warriors.

The order has come down from on high that when out patrolling the stricken streets of the city of Port-au-Prince, the paratroopers should have their rifles slung behind their backs. None of that strong-arm brandishing of metal that epitomised the early days in Iraq. "We've been told not to draw attention to our guns," the paratrooper, Sgt David Gurba, said.

By Monday, the US military was visibly out in force at the main airport in Port-au-Prince. Two mammoth C17 military transport aircraft were on the tarmac, one of which landed in front of us, the other unloading jeeps and armoured vehicles.

Providing a solid background hum, the Black Hawks moved in and out of the airport every five minutes, swinging round from the airport to the USS Carl Vinson where 30 of the helicopters were based.

There are 1,700 US troops here, substantially less than the 5,000 or so that had been promised by now.

But in the next couple of days, 2,200 reinforcements from the 22nd Marine Expeditionary Unit, backed up by amphibious units, are scheduled to arrive. By mid-week, the US military says, it will have up to 5,000 personnel on the ground and a similar number at sea.

Earthquake victims desperate for aid run toward a US helicopter making a water drop near a country club being used as an operating base in Port-au-Prince, Haiti. (© AP Images/Jae C. Hong.)

You can't move such numbers of US soldiers into a sovereign country without it looking, slightly inevitably, like an invasion. But that's an impression the Americans are hyper-sensitive about countering. Whoever we talked to made a point of repeating that paratrooper's message.

The US Military's Focus Is Humanitarian Aid

"I cannot say this more clearly," the spokesman for the commander of the joint task force told us, standing on the tarmac in his military fatigues. "The focus of the American presence on the ground is to help with the humanitarian work. Obama, as our commander-in-chief, has given us the mission of alleviating suffering as much as we can, as fast as we can."

Over at the US embassy on the outskirts of the city, the same message was delivered even more directly:

"This is a primary concern of ours," the embassy spokesman told us. "We want the people of Haiti to understand that we are here to help. We are not here to invade or occupy."

The desire to avoid any semblance of invasion is understandable, given the past few years in Afghanistan and Iraq. But there's also a local sensitivity, born of wave upon wave of American interference in the internal affairs of Haiti. Interference that Haitians have put behind them, but that they will never forget.

The Haitian in whose house in Port-au-Prince we are staying—a prominent businessman and generally very pro-America—keeps a cherished machete on his wall. It was used, he explained to me one night, by his grandfather to attack US soldiers during the 1915–1934 American occupation of his country.

"This is a UN-led mission," the US spokesman for the joint task force said. "We are just one of many countries that are contributing to the rescue mission."

Americans Act with Caution

Such sensitivities perhaps go some way to explain why the American aid effort in Haiti has so far been so cautious. Day seven of the catastrophe, yet wherever we go we are still surrounded by crowds of people living on the streets pleading with us for water. A few miles away at the airport, huge quantities of supplies are stacked high in the sun. Under a deal finalised between the heads of relevant parties on Sunday night, US troops will be responsible for securing the incoming supplies at the airport, and then moving them to four central distribution hubs. One of those hubs is at the national football stadium in downtown Port-au-Prince and another at a golf course near the US embassy.

That will free up troops from the UN peacekeeping force in Haiti, so the official line goes, to take charge of the next stage of the process—getting the aid out of the central hubs and to the neighbourhoods. For that purpose the UN has pinpointed 14 distribution locations where it, together with aid groups, will hand out the goods.

The plan sounds neat, thoroughly thought-out, foolproof. There is only one problem: it is several days late.

Only on Monday were those supplies stranded at the airport beginning to be moved to the four central hubs, and they still need to reach the 14 distribution points, and in turn get given out to the bewildered, sunken people.

Haitians Welcome the Americans

Given that, it's remarkable how patient people appear. In contrast to the lurid accounts of looting and lynching—which has happened, albeit sporadically and at localised flashpoints—the Haitians remain strikingly welcoming of the Americans.

> The Haitians remain strikingly welcoming of the Americans.

"The people have been amazingly peaceful in the circumstances," said Sgt Ryan McGee, one of the paratroopers at the airport, who has been out in the city on security details. "We've seen a little bit of violence in places. But generally wherever we've shown up people have cheered us on. 'USA Number One!'"

On our drive to the airport, we pass one of the myriad piles of rubble where men are still scratching away with pick axes in the now fading hope of finding further survivors. The sight has become so common, so ingrained in the senses, that you hardly notice anymore scenes of astonishing destruction.

And then we did notice. On top of one pile, leading the digging, there was a man with his arms crossed. He was wearing a dusty, crooked Uncle Sam hat.

US Troops Pack to Leave Haiti

USA Today

In the following viewpoint, writers from the American daily news-paper *USA Today* describe the departure of US troops from Haiti. US troops helped to secure the airport and distribute aid as well as treating the wounded. They also provided security. There was criticism about the role of US troops from some Haitian quarters, due to the unpleasant memories of previous American intervention and occupation of Haiti. However, according to the writers, most Haitians were glad for the help and sorry to see the Americans leave.

Port-au-Prince, Haiti (AP)—U.S. troops are with-drawing from the shattered capital, leaving many Haitians anxious that the most visible portion of international relief is ending even as the city is still mired in misery and vulnerable to unrest.

As troops packed their duffels and began to fly home this weekend, Haitians and some aid workers wondered

SOURCE. "US Troops Pack to Leave Haiti," *USA Today*, March 7, 2010, p. 4. Reprinted with permission of the Associated Press.

A man greets a US soldier along the earthquake-torn streets of downtown Port-au-Prince, Haiti. Thousands of people were still displaced when US troops began departing Haiti in March 2010. (© Marco Dormino/MINUSTAH via Getty Images.)

whether U.N. peacekeepers and local police are up to the task of maintaining order. More than a half-million people still live in vast encampments that have grown more unpleasant in recent days with the early onset of rainy season.

Some also fear the departure of the American troops is a sign of dwindling international interest in the plight of the Haitian people following the catastrophic Jan. 12 earthquake.

"I would like for them to stay in Haiti until they rebuild the country and everybody can go back to their house," said Marjorie Louis, a 27-year-old mother of two, as she warmed a bowl of beans for her family over a charcoal fire on the fake grass of the national stadium.

U.S. officials say the long-anticipated draw down of troops is not a sign of waning commitment to Haiti, only a change in the nature of the operation. Security will now be the responsibility of the 10,000-strong U.N. peacekeeping force and the Haitian police.

A smaller number of U.S. forces—the exact number has not yet been determined—will be needed as the U.N. and Haitian government reassert control, said Gen. Douglas Fraser, head of U.S. Southern Command, which runs the Haiti operation.

"Our mission is largely accomplished," Fraser said.

American forces arrived in the immediate aftermath of the quake to treat the wounded, provide emergency water and rations and help prevent a feared outbreak of violence among desperate survivors. They also helped reopen the airport and seaport.

> The military operation was criticized by some Haitian senators and foreign leaders as heavy-handed and inappropriate.

There has been no widespread violence but security is a real issue. A U.N. food convoy traveling from Gonaives to Dessalines on Friday was stopped and overrun by people, who looted two trucks before peacekeepers regained control, U.N. officials said.

They managed to escort the other two back to Gonaives. There were no reports of injuries.

The military operation was criticized by some Haitian senators and foreign leaders as heavy-handed and inappropriate in a country that had been occupied by American forces for nearly two decades in the early 20th century. But ordinary Haitians largely welcomed the troops, many out of disenchantment with their own government.

"They should stay because they have been doing a good job," 35-year-old Lesly Pierre said as his family prepared dinner under a tarp at an encampment in Petion-ville. "If it was up to our government, we wouldn't have gotten any help at all."

U.S. soldiers said they had nothing but warm encounters with the Haitian people.

"They're real good people. They just want help," Army Private First Class Troy Sims, a 19-year-old from Fresno,

California, said as he prepared to board a flight back to the U.S. "I feel that us being here helped a lot. If we weren't here, things probably would have gotten out of control."

There are now about 11,000 troops, more than half of them on ships just off the coast, down from a peak of around 20,000 on Feb. 1. The total is expected to drop to about 8,000 in coming days as the withdrawal gathers steam. The military said more than 700 paratroopers left this weekend.

Soldiers are now gone from the General Hospital, where they once directed traffic and kept order amid the chaos of mass casualties. There are no more Haitian patients on board the USNS Comfort, which treated 8,600 people after the quake. At a country club in Petionville, where some 100,000 Haitians are living in rough shelters in a muddy ravine, only a few soldiers remain of the several hundred there after the disaster.

Alison Thompson said she was nervous about the smaller U.S. troop contingent.

"Soon we are not going to have any security," said Thompson, medical coordinator of the Jenkins/Penn Relief Organization, which runs a field hospital at the edge of the ravine. "Everybody is just so worried that they are pulling out because it's going to get dangerous."

It was the same concern for Louis at the national stadium.

"If the troublemakers see that there is some kind of force here, they will think twice before they do anything," she said. "They are already getting ready to stir up trouble."

But Ted Constan, chief program officer for Partners in Health, said that the way to address security is to get adequate shelter and other aid to the hundreds of thousands of people who are now stranded in squalid encampments.

"The real solution is to deliver services . . . rather than turn Haiti into a military state," he said.

Crime and Violence Increase in the Months After the Earthquake

Louis-Alexandre Berg

In the following viewpoint, US Institute of Peace scholar Louis-Alexandre Berg reports on the rise of crime and violence in Haiti in the months following the earthquake. He attributes this rise to the escape of so many prisoners from jail, as well as to the growth of gangs. In addition, political upheaval and graft contributed to the lawlessness. The large number of people living in tent camps because of the destruction of their homes fostered crime as well. Berg is a rule of law adviser at the United States Agency for International Development.

S ince the earthquake on January 12, 2010, worldwide attention has focused on rebuilding Haiti's physical infrastructure and governance capacity.

Women Are the Target of Post-Earthquake Violence

Protection mechanisms for women and girl victims of sexual violence were deficient before the earthquake, now they are totally absent. This is a major cause for under-reporting. The Courts of the Peace were not operational at the time of writing and their new temporary locations were still unknown. Police stations that remain operational did not have adequate facilities for women to file complaints safely and confidentially. For example, the Port-au-Prince police station, situated in Champ de Mars, hosts one of the few units set up to respond to violence against women. Since the destruction of the station, it is reduced to a dusty table on the pavement located just in front of the police cells and exposed to passersby. . . .

Amnesty International documented cases of sexual violence in camps. Four of the victims interviewed were children. An 8-year-old girl called Celine (not her real name) was alone in the tent at night when she was raped. Her mother had left the camp to work and had no one to look after her daughter during her absence. A 15-year-old girl, called Fabienne (not her real name) was raped when she left the camp to urinate, as there were no latrines within the camp. Carline (not her real name), 21, was raped by 3 men when she went to urinate in a remote area of the camp, as the latrines were too dirty to be used. Pascaline (not her real name), 21, was raped and beaten in her tent, neighbors failed to intervene because they believed she was with her partner.

SOURCE. *Amnesty International,* Haiti: After the Earthquake, *March 2010. www .amnesty.org.*

This already monumental task is complicated by the risk that Haiti's prior cycles of crime, violence or instability may re-emerge to disrupt the reconstruction process. Although violent crime has decreased since its height in 2005, the earthquake has created new vulnerabilities and fueled an increase in crime. If not properly managed, these risks could threaten the upcoming elections and reconstruction process.

Crime and Violence Are on the Rise

Since the devastating earthquake in January, criminal activity has increased in parts of Port-au-Prince, fueling fears of renewed instability and violence throughout the city. The rise in crime is driven largely by the escape of thousands of prisoners from the National Penitentiary in Port-au-Prince following the earthquake. According to the Haitian National Police (HNP), 5,136 prisoners escaped, including around 700 violent gang members. Some of these escapees have accessed hidden caches of weapons. As of mid-July, only 627 had been recaptured, including roughly 100 gang members, although more were being rounded up daily.

This massive escape has set off a new wave of crime, especially in the most vulnerable areas. Many gang members have sought to return to their former neighborhoods, setting off violent turf battles and increased street crime. A new armed group known as the *Armee Federale* has brought together the escaped prisoners from several neighborhoods. They hide out in the hills of the Martissant section of Port-au-Prince and conduct increasingly organized criminal activities throughout the city. Cases of kidnapping and assault increased during the first half of 2010 and crime has been reported in the previously quiet suburbs above Port-au-Prince.

> The proliferation of displaced people in tent camps around the city has created an additional burden for the security forces.

This increase in crime has been compounded by damage to an already weak HNP and justice system. Faced with 79 deaths and hundreds of injuries among their ranks, police officers were initially absorbed with the post-earthquake clean up, leading to an immediate reduction in the effective force by around half. The numbers have since risen to the pre-earthquake level of roughly 9,000, yet many HNP continue to operate out of tents next to destroyed stations, while over 65 percent of vehicles and much of their equipment remains damaged or destroyed. The U.N. mission (MINUSTAH) also sustained significant damage that temporarily affected its capacity until its ranks were replenished.

The proliferation of displaced people in tent camps around the city has created an additional burden for the security forces and an opportunity for criminals. Humanitarian agencies have succeeded in averting widespread epidemics and famine among the estimated 1.9 million people displaced by the earthquake, by distributing tents, food, water and medical care. Yet, the tent camps set up in hundreds of places around the city are vulnerable not only to disease and the elements, but also to violence. The U.N. has identified numerous cases of thefts, rapes and domestic violence within camps and camp residents continue to report a high level of insecurity. Residents also report that escaped prisoners have been using the camps as safe havens, and the police hesitate to enter the camps in pursuit of criminals for fear of civilian casualties. Many camps have set up "security committees," but these groups lack training or clear channels of communication with either camp residents or the police.

Political Conflict During Elections Could Fuel Further Violence

With elections approaching, increased gang activity may be linked to political struggles. Although reduced political tensions in the early days of the [Hatian president René] Préval government weakened the link between crime and politics, political conflict is now on the rise. The government is planning to hold presidential and parliamentary elections in November 2010 to meet the constitutional timeframe for the new government to take office. Opposition leaders, however, have accused the government of stacking the elections against them. Several parties are calling for mass mobilization in an effort to force Préval to step down and change the composition of the Provisional Election Commission. Attendance at demonstrations has been limited so far, but even minor incidents of violence could easily disrupt the elections process. In this climate, unemployed youth and reinvigorated gangs seeking to re-establish their turf may be a tempting target for political leaders seeking to mobilize demonstrators, disrupt the elections or undermine the government after the elections.

Port-au-Prince Gangs Arose from Divisive Politics and Weak Governance

The link between neighborhood youth groups, armed gangs and political conflict is rooted in Haiti's winner-take-all politics, in which the use of informal armed groups has been a long-favored political strategy, fueled by widespread poverty, weak government services and deep social and economic inequities. Youth gangs are based in the poorest and most marginalized urban neighborhoods in Port-au-Prince and in other urban areas around the country. The growing youth population in these areas was vulnerable to the tumultuous social and political forces around them. In the early 1990s, these neighborhoods became politically active, largely in support of President Jean-Bertrand Aristide, who promised to focus on their plight after decades of neglect. Both Aristide and his political rivals sought to build upon this support, distributing weapons to groups of youth and mobilizing them to protect their political and economic interests. These groups assumed responsibility for security in their neighborhoods, often extorting market sellers and other businesses in exchange for protection, and sometimes becoming involved in drug smuggling and other illicit activities.

Violent turf battles intensified after Aristide's departure as armed groups competed for control of neighborhoods and money-making opportunities. In the run-up to the 2006 elections, political parties and private sector actors exploited these divisions, distributing cash and weapons to armed groups in exchange for their assistance in mobilizing people to demonstrate and vote for them, to disrupt the elections, or to protect their businesses. Some groups linked up with organized criminal enterprises—involving kidnapping, arms trading and drug smuggling—to bring in revenue and to raise their profile politically in bids for external support. Other groups remained localized, driven by violent rivalries specific to each neighborhood. As kidnapping and murders spread throughout Port-au-Prince, nowhere did people suffer more than within the underprivileged neighborhoods where the armed groups were based. Children were recruited to carry weapons and drugs, women were raped and kidnapped as sex slaves, and innocent civilians were caught in the crossfire of gang wars and turf battles.

Fragile Steps Toward Stability Before the Earthquake

The level of crime declined significantly after 2006 due to an evolving political context, robust operations by MINUSTAH and the HNP, and increased investment in marginalized neighborhoods. After his election in 2006, President René Préval calmed tensions by reaching out to many of the country's political factions and bringing them into his coalition, thereby reducing incentives for political violence. He established relationships with gang leaders, reportedly promising them jobs and resources in exchange for ending their criminal activities. In 2007, the failure of these negotiations amidst continuing crime led Préval to support a series of combined MINUSTAH and HNP operations in Cite Soleil that captured or forced into exile many of the top gang leaders.

At the same time, donor-funded programs enhanced the availability of services and infrastructure in these

neighborhoods and improved relationships between the population and local authorities. For example, the U.S.-sponsored Haiti Stabilization Initiative (HSI) combined short-term jobs, infrastructure, and support to the HNP to create a more conducive atmosphere for development projects and private-sector investment. Other projects supported dialogue and community-building to reduce tensions across rival neighborhoods.

The security situation throughout Port-au-Prince improved. With their leadership disrupted, armed groups decreased in size and could no longer carry out organized operations like kidnapping. Political tensions

Police officers patrol in Port-au-Prince, Haiti, in April 2010, as people sit outside their homes to eat. During this time, the police were attempting to control the crime in the vast slums created by the earthquake. (© AP Images/Ramon Espinosa.)

became less salient, and turf battles decreased in intensity. The HNP expanded their presence in some neighborhoods and public confidence in them improved as efforts at professionalizing the HNP began to take root. Improvements in infrastructure—most notably two new police stations and an expanded main road through Cite Soleil—contributed to improved relationships among residents and government authorities.

Nonetheless, armed groups continued to operate and prey on the people within their communities, primarily through petty, neighborhood-level crimes. While some neighborhoods benefited from donor projects, others were left out, fueling continued tensions. In a mere three years, donor attention to these areas did not translate into sufficient new jobs, government services, or sense of community, while the sense of exclusion among residents of these neighborhoods remained high.

> Overcrowded urban areas plagued by high poverty and unemployment combined with weak government institutions will continue to serve as breeding grounds for violent crime.

In the aftermath of the earthquake, these fragile improvements were set back as escaped prisoners returned to their neighborhoods, law enforcement capabilities weakened, and the intensive focus on marginalized areas waned, allowing violent crime to re-emerge. The HNP and MINUSTAH have stepped up their presence in camps and staged high profile operations in search of escaped prisoners. As the justice system struggles to function after the destruction to buildings, files and personnel, these large-scale operations risk raising the already high number of pre-trial detainees. Meanwhile, camp residents continue to report that they rarely see the overstretched and under-resourced HNP, residents of slum areas report decreased confidence in the police, and security across the city has declined.

Community Development, Services, Jobs, and Law Enforcement Will Decrease Violence

The increase in insecurity since the earthquake underscores Haiti's continued vulnerability to violent crime and political instability. Overcrowded urban areas plagued by high poverty and unemployment combined with weak government institutions will continue to serve as breeding grounds for violent crime and armed groups for years to come. As political conflict escalates, these groups can be manipulated by political or economic interests to fuel broader instability.

Efforts that had begun to demonstrate progress in addressing these challenges prior to the earthquake should be continued and expanded. The combination of improved infrastructure, government services in marginalized areas inside and outside of Port-au-Prince, jobs and education for at-risk youth, and robust law enforcement can reduce the propensity toward violence in these areas, if they are sustained for sufficient time and linked to longer-term development. Critical to these efforts is a focus on improving social ties within and across communities to reduce tension, and building local capacity for managing conflicts. Improvements to the management and leadership of the HNP, implementing stalled reforms in the judiciary, strengthening local government, and fostering dialogue and reconciliation among political parties are further necessary to avoid recurrent crime and political conflict. As they turn their attention from immediate humanitarian aid toward reconstruction, the Haitian government and international community should direct resources toward mitigating conflict in the short-term while continuing to address the underlying drivers of crime and violence in Haiti.

CHAPTER 2

Controversies Surrounding the Haiti Earthquake

Haiti Gives Conflicting Count for Quake Deaths

Michelle Faul

In the following viewpoint, Associated Press journalist Michelle Faul reports on the conflicting death tolls offered by Haitian government officials. The discrepancies led to doubts about the accuracy of reports and skepticism on the part of international aid agencies concerning the actual death toll. On one hand, a large death toll meant more humanitarian aid dollars; on the other, an inflated death toll would turn off potential donors.

Photo on previous page: A camp was set up for displaced victims in this airstrip in Port-au-Prince, Haiti. Hundreds of thousands of people were still living in vast tent cities many months after the earthquake. (© AP Images/Ramon Espinosa.)

Haiti issued wildly conflicting death tolls for the Jan. 12 earthquake on Wednesday, adding to confusion about how many people actually died—and to suspicion that nobody really knows.

A day after Communications Minister Marie-Laurence Jocelyn Lassegue raised the official death toll to 230,000, her office put out a statement quoting President Rene Preval as saying 270,000 bodies had

SOURCE. Michelle Faul, "Haiti Gives Conflicting Count for Quake Deaths," Associated Press, February 10, 2010. Reprinted with permission of the Associated Press.

been hastily buried by the government following the earthquake. A press officer withdrew the statement, saying there was an error, but re-issued it within minutes. Later Wednesday, the ministry said that due to a typo, the number should have read 170,000.

Even that didn't clear things up. In the late afternoon, Preval and Lassegue appeared together at the government's temporary headquarters.

Preval, speaking English, told journalists that the number was 170,000, apparently referring to the number of bodies contained in mass graves.

Lassegue interrupted him in French, giving a number lower than she had given the previous day: "No, no, the official number is 210,000."

Preval dismissed her.

"Oh, she doesn't know what she's talking about," he said, again in English.

Whatever the death toll, there is no doubt it is one of the highest in a modern disaster.

A third of Haiti's 9 million people were crowded into the chaotic capital when the quake struck just to the southwest a few minutes before 5 P.M. Many were preparing to leave their offices or schools. Some 250,000 houses and 30,000 commercial buildings collapsed, according to government estimates, many crushing people inside.

For days, people piled bodies by the side of the road or left them half-buried under the rubble. Countless more remain under collapsed buildings, identified only by a pungent odor.

No foreign government or independent agency has issued its own death toll. Many agencies that usually can help estimate casualty numbers say they are too busy helping the living to keep track of the dead. And the Joint Task Force in charge of the relief effort—foreign governments and militaries, U.N. agencies and Haitian government officials—quotes only the government death toll.

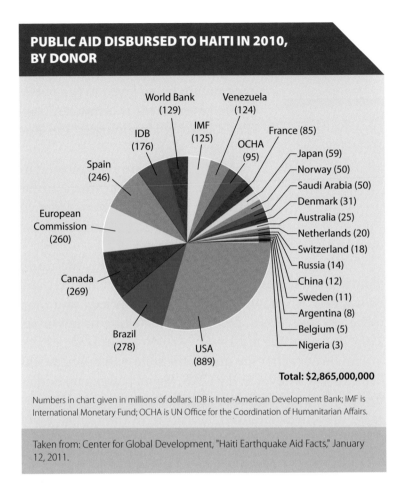

PUBLIC AID DISBURSED TO HAITI IN 2010, BY DONOR

World Bank (129)
Venezuela (124)
IMF (125)
IDB (176)
OCHA (95)
France (85)
Japan (59)
Norway (50)
Saudi Arabia (50)
Spain (246)
Denmark (31)
Australia (25)
European Commission (260)
Netherlands (20)
Switzerland (18)
Russia (14)
Canada (269)
China (12)
Sweden (11)
Argentina (8)
Brazil (278)
Belgium (5)
USA (889)
Nigeria (3)

Total: $2,865,000,000

Numbers in chart given in millions of dollars. IDB is Inter-American Development Bank; IMF is International Monetary Fund; OCHA is UN Office for the Coordination of Humanitarian Affairs.

Taken from: Center for Global Development, "Haiti Earthquake Aid Facts," January 12, 2011.

That toll has climbed from a precise 111,481 on Jan. 23 to 150,000 on Jan. 24, to 212,000 on Saturday, to 230,000 on Tuesday. Preval's count of 170,000 bodies buried in mass graves may represent only a piece of the toll—but nobody at his office was available to clarify.

It's common in major disasters to see large discrepancies in death tolls: Governments may use lower figures to save face, or higher figures to attract foreign aid. In Haiti's case, however, where the very institutions responsible for compiling information were themselves devastated, reaching a death toll is particularly difficult.

Even some officials express skepticism that the government is keeping count.

"I personally think that a lot of information being given to the public by the government is estimates," said Haiti's chief epidemiologist, Dr. Roc Magloire.

> Many citizens [accuse] the government of inflating the numbers to attract foreign aid.

Many citizens are even more cynical, accusing the government of inflating the numbers to attract foreign aid and to take the spotlight off its own lackluster response to the disaster.

"Nobody knows how they came up with the death count. There's no list of names. No list of who may still be trapped. No pictures of people they buried," said shop owner Jacques Desal, 45. "No one is telling us anything. They just want the aid."

A few days after the quake, the state-run public works department, known as the CNE, began picking up bodies from the streets and dropping them in trenches dug by earth movers in Titanyen, just north of the capital, amid rolling chalk and limestone hills that overlook the Caribbean Sea.

The trenches are 6 meters (20 feet) deep and piled 6 meters (20 feet) high.

Preval said the government has counted 170,000 bodies during those efforts, and that the number does not include people buried in private ceremonies. But at Titanyen on Wednesday, worker Estelhomme Saint Val said nobody had counted the bodies.

"The trucks were just dropping people wherever, and then we would move in and cover them up," he said. "We buried people all along the roads and roadsides. It was impossible to do a count."

And although the government death toll jumped by the thousands from Saturday to Tuesday, Saint Val said at noon Wednesday that only one truck had arrived this

week, and it carried two bodies. He said workers received 15 truckloads of bodies a day just after the quake, but the numbers dropped off about 10 days ago.

Lassegue, in announcing the Tuesday death toll, refused to say how it was calculated.

"For the moment we count 230,000 deaths, but these figures are not definitive," she said, "it's a partial figure."

U.N. humanitarian spokeswoman Elisabeth Byrs in Geneva, who has often cited Haitian government figures, said Wednesday that she said she doesn't know how Haiti is calculating the death toll: "We cannot confirm these figures."

Finding someone who can is difficult.

The government says the CNE is orchestrating the count. The CNE referred questions to the prime minister's office. The prime minister's chief of protocol referred questions to the prime minister's secretary-general. The prime minister's secretary-general could not be reached.

The day after the earthquake, people search for survivors in a collapsed building using sledgehammers and other tools. The search for survivors was extremely difficult and complicated efforts to calculate the number of dead. (© AP Images/ Ricardo Arduengo.)

A report by the U.N. on Tuesday attributed the death toll to Haiti's Civil Protection Agency instead of the CNE. Civil Protection director Alta Jean-Baptiste referred questions to the Ministry of Interior. Interior Minister Paul Antoine Bien-Aime said Wednesday that the Civil Protection toll is "217,000-and-some deaths," despite the higher number given by his government.

"Civil Protection, before giving out the numbers, really is doing a precise count and the numbers that they give out are numbers that are proven," he said.

He would not say how that count is being done.

A death toll of 230,000 would equal the number of people killed in the tsunami that devastated a dozen countries around the Indian Ocean following a magnitude-9.2 earthquake on Dec. 26, 2004. That disaster generated an outpouring of international aid—in part because of the number of dead.

An extremely high toll "probably elicits more public sympathy, so it might generate more visibility, more funding," said Chris Lorn, a spokesman for the International Organization for Migration.

But Byrs says inflating numbers can backfire.

"Regarding every estimate, we have to be very careful because we could lose credibility with donors, with humanitarian partners," she told The Associated Press. "If you boost the figure, it's counterproductive. It doesn't help when you try to match assistance to needs."

A Controversial Report Dramatically Lowers the Estimated Cost of the Haiti Earthquake

Guy Adams

In the following viewpoint, Guy Adams, a journalist who writes for the *Irish Independent*, reports on the controversy over the death toll from the Haiti earthquake. He describes a report commissioned by the United States Agency of International Development (USAID) that placed the death count at much lower than Haitian officials asserted. The report generated significant controversy because it suggested to foreign donors that Haitian governmental figures were inflating the death count to increase monetary aid in order to line their own pockets. At the same time, questions concerning the integrity of the report were raised.

SOURCE. Guy Adams, "Cock-up or Conspiracy? Rift Opens Over Real Cost of Haiti Earthquake," *Independent*, June 1, 2011. Copyright © 2011 Independent Newspapers (UK) Ltd. Reproduced by permission.

It was called the worst disaster in modern history. A UN spokesman described "historic" devastation "like no other" ever faced by the organisation.

News reports heralded scenes of Biblical devastation, complete with piles of corpses in the streets and lorry-loads of bodies being dumped in graves on the outskirts of town.

But how many people really did lose their lives when an earthquake measuring 7.0 on the Richter Scale struck Haiti on January 12, 2010? Was the death toll in the tens of thousands, or hundreds of thousands? And did a mixture of cock-up and conspiracy result in the scale of destruction being dramatically overstated?

A Much Lower Death Toll

The US Agency for International Development (USAID) seems to think so. In a leaked report, the organisation has concluded that the actual number of deaths in last year's disaster was somewhere between 46,000 and 85,000, well short of the estimates of between 200,000 and 300,000 made by most aid groups, and a fraction of the 318,000 claimed by the Haitian government.

Numbers matter, because they help to justify the vast and ongoing aid effort in which around $5.5bn [USD] (€3.8bn) has been pledged to the impoverished Caribbean nation by overseas governments. The numbers also continue to inspire private donations to the roughly 3,000 charities and aid agencies which are still invested there.

The US report has not yet been published, but its alleged findings have already been disputed by both Haitian authorities and the UN. Even the State Department in Washington is, for now, reluctant to endorse it, saying that "internal inconsistencies" in some of the statistical analysis are currently being investigated prior to publication.

"We are reviewing these inconsistencies . . . to ensure information we release is accurate," spokeswoman Preeti Shah said.

The USAID Report Disputes Haitian Statistics

The draft was compiled for USAID by a private consulting firm, LTL Strategies, which claims to have arrived at its revised death toll by conducting extended interviews in 5,200 homes in Port-au-Prince earlier this year. Respondents were asked more than 100 questions, including how many people died in each building, and where the survivors went. As well as concluding that the death toll was exaggerated, the report claims the number of people made homeless by the disaster—originally estimated at 1.5 million by the UN—was in fact 895,000. And while UN officials estimate that 680,000 Haitians are still living in temporary settlement camps, the real figure is closer to 375,000, the report concludes.

One year after the earthquake, the Port-au-Prince cathedral still lies in ruins. (© Carl Juste/MCT via Getty Images.)

HOW MANY REALLY DIED IN THE HAITI EARTHQUAKE?

Time line of death toll estimates

Date	Information Source	Estimated Number of Dead
2010		
January 14	Haitian president René Préval	30,000–50,000
January 16	Red Cross	45,000–50,000
	Pan American Development Foundation	50,000–100,000
January 23	Haitian government	111,481
January 24	Haitian government	150,000
	United Nations	112,350
January 31	Haitian government	212,000
February 3	Haitian Ministry of Communications	230,000
	Haitian president René Préval	270,000
February 4	Haitian Ministry of Communications	170,000–270,000 (Ministry announces typo in previous estimate and that the death toll is estimated at 170,000; but also says that they are currently counting the death toll as 270,000)
February 15	Haitian Civil Protection Service	217,366
February 21	Haitian president René Préval	300,000
February 23	Netherlands Radio Worldwide	92,000
2011		
May 30	United States Agency for International Development	46,000–85,000

Compiled by editor.

A third key finding suggests that the amount of rubble produced by the quake, which the US Army Corps of Engineers put at 20 million cubic metres, is in fact less than half that amount. The expensive fleet of lorries still working to clear ruins may therefore be finished sooner than previously thought.

> Haiti's government has never revealed the methodology behind its figures. And . . . they are impossible to confirm.

The report has the potential to be hugely controversial, since it speaks directly to concerns that international relief efforts create a culture of dependency and corruption. Haiti is already often cited as proof that disasters, and the overseas aid spending they prompt, are all too easily exploited by dishonest locals.

The official death toll has always been eye-opening, since at 318,000, it represents roughly 3 percent of the entire population of Haiti. Many wondered how officials were able to release precise figures throughout the initial weeks of the catastrophe, even as bodies were being scooped haphazardly off the streets and dumped in mass graves.

Haiti's government has never revealed the methodology behind its figures. And since the majority of public records were destroyed during the quake, they are impossible to confirm. Anyone who was in Haiti during January 2010 can of course attest to the horrifying scale of suffering. In some areas, corpses were piled high on pavements. Field hospitals were overwhelmed, and nearly everyone you spoke to seemed to have lost at least one member of their immediate family.

Enumerating that suffering is not an exact science, though. The UN, for example, lost 96—roughly 1.4 per cent—of its 7,000 peacekeepers in the country. If the same proportion were to be applied to the entire population of Haiti—10 million—then one might estimate that

140,000 people would have been killed. But UN peace-keepers living in well-built compounds could expect to have had a far higher survival rate than impoverished slum-dwellers who had constructed their homes out of breeze blocks.

As the leaked USAID report is the result of formal research, questions are already being asked as to its integrity. The 5,000 or so people whom researchers surveyed all came from Port-au-Prince, critics have noted. But some of the worst-hit locations were outside the capital.

A US Researcher Defends His Calculation of the Haiti Earthquake Death Toll

Timothy Schwartz

In the following viewpoint, researcher Timothy Schwarz defends the methodology he used to compile a report on the Haiti earthquake death toll for the United States Agency for International Development. He reviews the estimates made by various Haitian officials, demonstrating the wild fluctuation in numbers and the lack of evidence to support the claims. His own figures, he asserts, are based on solid research and evidence. Schwartz is the author of *Travesty in Haiti: A True Account of Christian Missions, Orphanages, Fraud, Food Aid and Drug Trafficking.*

This is a response to a report that I wrote for USAID [United States Agency for International Development] regarding the Haiti earthquake death toll. I don't know if I am even free to discuss the report because it's not official yet. However, what I can do is discuss the validity of the Haiti earthquake death toll count and whether or not a low death toll estimate should come as a surprise. The answer is "no," it should not be a surprise, not to anyone in Haiti. Here's a review of how the government arrived at the death toll and summary of data I compiled from elsewhere and that bears on the death toll.

Haiti Government Death Toll Estimates

On the 14th of January, day two after the Earthquake, President [René] Préval said that estimates of the number dead ranged from 30,000 to 50,000 but concluded that, "It's too early to give a number."

On the 16th of January the Red Cross estimated 45,000 to 50,000 dead and PADF [Pan American Development Foundation] 50,000 to 100,000. They based it on their volunteers. . . .

The very next day, the government tripled the number, issuing an official declaration of 140,000 dead.

On the 23rd, after Belgian disaster response expert Claude de Ville de Goyet noted that "round numbers are a sure sign that nobody knows." The government almost immediately offered a precise figure of 111,481 dead.

But on the next day, January 24th, they upped the figure to an even 150,000 killed, an increase of 38,000 over the day before. The same day, Secretary-General Edmund Mulet of the UN Stabilization Mission in Haiti, put the figure at 112,350 dead, 194,000 injured. It was not clear what he based his estimate on.

One week later, on Saturday the 31st, the Haitian government added a rather exact 100,000 to the UN figure, saying the death toll was 212,000.

The remains of victims in Port-au-Prince, Haiti, are loaded on the back of a truck. The collection of bodies was not carefully supervised to provide an accurate death count from the earthquake. (© Joe Raedle/Getty Images.)

Three days later, Wednesday February 3rd, Ministry of Communications raised the official death toll to 230,000 and then President René Préval added another 40,000 to the count, saying that the government had buried 270,000 bodies.

Confusing Information

When Michelle Faul of the AP [Associated Press] called and inquired regarding how the government was arriving at its figures, the press secretary withdrew the statement, saying there was an error. Within minutes it was re-issued.

The next day, under pressure to explain, the ministry again said that it was a typo, the number should have read 170,000. But in the same conversation the Minister concluded that, "For the moment we count 230,000 deaths"—60,000 more than she had said the day before. But even that was not definitive, "It's a partial figure."

When Michelle Faul tried to figure out how they arrived at the new figures, she was told that the government organization CNE [National Center for Equipment] was counting. CNE officials referred questions to the prime minister's office. The prime minister's office referred questions to the Prime Minister's Secretary-General. The Prime Minister's Secretary-General could not be reached. Someone along the way said that it was not CNE that was counting, it was CP (Civil Protection). CP director Alta Jean-Baptiste referred questions to Ministry of Interior Antoine Bien-Aime who assured Faul that, "CP is doing a precise count and the numbers they give out are numbers that are proven." When Faul asked how they arrived at the numbers, he couldn't say.

When Faul went out to the government sites, CNE drivers and workers told her that, "no one has been keeping tabs." One of the workers told her that, "The trucks were just dropping people wherever, and then we would move in and cover them up. . . . It was impossible to do a count."

Assad Volcy, a spokesman for the National Palace, tried to clear matters up. "Experts" he said, had devised a formula to calculate how many quake victims have been buried. When asked what that formula was, Volcy said he didn't know.

On the 15th of February, CP officially declared 217,366 people died from the 12 January earthquake. They also said that 1,301,491 people were living in tent cities.

The only news agency to ever question the death count issue again was Netherlands Radio Worldwide, whose journalists carefully checked all the Government sources, visiting cemeteries and burial grounds, and concluded on February 23rd that even if 30,000 people were still under the rubble and another 10,000 disposed of privately or burned, there were still no more than 92,000 people killed and probably less. They pointed to gross inconsistencies, such as that the Central government reported 20,000 to 30,000 deaths in Leogane, while local Leogane authorities claimed to have buried 3,364 (two weeks after the earthquake they had told me 1,600). The Central government also claimed 4,000 dead in Jacmel, while local Jacmel authorities reported 300 to 400 dead (ACTED, a French NGO [non-governmental organization] whose workers were involved in burying the dead, reported 145).

On February 21, President Préval raised the total body count to 300,000.

> It seems pretty clear that no one . . . had any idea how many people were killed.

Skewing the Numbers

It seems pretty clear that no one, not the government nor anyone else, had any idea how many people were killed. But the interesting thing is that, while I am not impugning any motivations, almost everyone who had anything to do with any type of official agency or NGO seemed deliberately bent on skewing the numbers as high as they possibly could. And they did so with total disregard for the evidence.

The UN—which on the anniversary of the earthquake posted on their website, "The quake killed more than 200,000 Haitians and left more than two million homeless"—lost 101 out of 9,151 international staff in Haiti at the time of the earthquake (1.1%). The US embassy, which also repeated the government death toll of over 200,000, lost 1 of 172 foreign staff members (0.58%) and 6 of 800 staff members (0.75%). Of the 43,000 US citizens and residents in Haiti at the time, the embassy was able to determine that 104 had been killed; 2,000 they could not locate (not unusual at the best of times). The Canadian Embassy reported losing 58 of 6,000 citizens in Haiti at the time (0.97%). The Dominicans lost 24 of 2,600 (0.92%), some 22 of whom were female sex workers who died in a single building.

The Haitian Government, which to this day issues varying claims of 17 to 30% of all civil servants killed, never has provided precise lists, not to anyone. The only thing we know for sure was that the parliament and the police were hit very hard. In the days after the earthquake, Mario Andresol, the Chief of Haiti's 8,000 member police force had said, "We lost 70 police officers, nearly 500 are still missing and 400 were wounded." When all was said and done, we know that 77 policemen were killed (that's 0.73% of the 10,544 police in Haiti), and if we figure that 80% are in Port-au-Prince—standard—then it's about 0.9% of those in Port-au-Prince were killed. We also know that two of 100 senators were killed and no congressman or ministers.

No More Questions

After the second or third week, journalists were no longer asking aid agencies about how many staff they had lost and the agencies were deferring to the Haitian Government for their figures. The United Nations, which had early on declared that it would come up with an official estimate, subsequently declined to conduct its own count. The Red Cross was mum. No other NGO ever questioned the figures again. On the contrary, as with the UN and the embassies, they invariably latched on to and restated the government figures.

In June 2010, the home page for Oxfam, which lost one of its 100 employees in Port-au-Prince at the time of the earthquake, was citing the government figure of 230,000; CRS [Catholic Relief Services] lost none of its 100 employees in Port-au-Prince but was citing the same figures; World Vision lost none of its 95 staff in Port-au-Prince but implied there were more, saying "at least 230,000 dead;" MSF [Médecins Sans Frontières/Doctors Without Borders] lost 7 of its staff of 800 but said the earthquake "killed hundreds of thousands of people." The Red Cross was the same, they lost no one. God's

Littlest Angels, featured on CBC, ABC, CNN, and Larry King, same, they lost no one either. Most NGOs lost no one. Businesses were the same: Triology lost 5 of 576 (0.9%); Digicel, 2 of 900 (0.02%); CEMEX, 0 of 115; Petion Ville Golf and Tennis Club 0 of 100, not a single employee even lost a home.

> At about 60,000 dead, that's still a huge tragedy.

Intellectually, I really don't care how many people got killed in the earthquake. The draft report for USAID was simply a job I was performing with a team of some 20 University educated professionals, including two other PhDs. But personally, for me, in terms of the tragedy, less is better. And at about 60,000 dead, that's still a huge tragedy.

The US Military Presence in Haiti Is an Unwelcome Invasion

Ezili Dantò

In the following viewpoint, Haitian writer and human rights law-
yer Ezili Dantò asserts that the US military presence in Haiti was
tantamount to an invasion, not the humanitarian effort claimed
by the US government. She further claims that the soldiers,
rather than helping, hindered rescue efforts by blocking true
first responders from the scene. Furthermore, they took over
functions rightfully belonging to the Haitian government. Dantò
calls for the Americans to go home.

The major media called on January 13, hours after
the earthquake ravaged Haiti. A black woman
working for a major TV station wanted to do a
special about Americans who go to Haiti and sacrifice

SOURCE. Ezili Dantò, "After the Earthquake, Haiti Can't Get a
Break," *Progressive*, March 24, 2010, pp. 24–28. progressive.org.
Reproduced by permission of The Progressive, 409 East Main Street,
Madison, WI 53703.

all to help the poor Haitians. "Can you help?" she asked. "My boss wants me to interview missionaries who give up electricity, comfort, and TV."

"You don't want to know what I have to say," I answered.

She got defensive. Said she was trying to change the narrative of the story. She told me she knew about false aid, false charity, false organized benevolence. She told me she understood that much of the NGO [nongovernmental organizations] humanitarian niche was corporate welfare on the backs of impoverished Haiti. But she had a job to do and maybe if I couldn't talk about helping the poor Haitians, being Haitian-born and all, maybe I could tell her who could.

I said, in all sincerity, there are those charity people who are conscientious and who have done a good job in Haiti. Call Partners in Health. They are legitimate because Haitians are trained to help themselves there, I said. But they probably won't meet the common story line you want because I assume you're looking to interview a white person, right? Or a black American? So you probably don't want to speak to the Haitian woman who runs Partners in Health in Haiti. Her name is Loune Viaud. If you want your story line, you'll have to bend things a bit and go to people she supervises. I'm sure you'll find a way to ignore Loune Viaud.

> Suddenly, we're very popular because black bodies are strewn on the streets of Port-au-Prince.

She hung up, saying she thought she could trust me to help her with Haiti because someone she knows suggested me.

A Media Bombardment

The media has called a lot since the earthquake.

Suddenly, we're very popular because black bodies are strewn on the streets of Port-au-Prince. Every

US MILITARY INTERVENTIONS AND OCCUPATIONS IN HAITI

1891	US troops sent to quell black revolt on Navassa Island.
1915–1934	US troops occupy Haiti for nineteen years, following revolt.
1994	Blockade against the military government of Haiti. US troops restore President Jean-Bertrand Aristide to power three years after his ouster by a military coup.
2004–2005	Marines occupy Haiti after Aristide is ousted again. Washington advises Aristide to leave the country.
2010	US troops provide humanitarian aid and security following Haiti earthquake.

Compiled by editor.

reporter who is somebody is rushing to take a picture. Oh, how terrible, terrible, they say.

The media called and lamented that the Haitian government was nowhere to be found.

The presidential palace collapsed, the police headquarters collapsed, the parliament building collapsed with legislators inside it, I say. No one knows how many policemen, municipal workers, legislators were there, how many escaped, or who was injured. Many government officials are looking for their loved ones. There's no communication, no telephones, no electricity, no roads in the capital that are passable, no water in many areas, the hospitals are damaged. Do you understand?

No one has heard in the immediate aftermath from the 9,000 U.N. troops in Haiti either, I further point out. They are mostly staying in their barracks, out of sight, or tending to their injured and dead also.

But the media is not concentrating on that, is it? Only on promoting, it seems, the standard line: *those-incompetent-Black-Haitians-can't-rule-themselves.*

Why doesn't Haiti get a break from that media bombardment? Not even now?

Haitians Are Desperate to Hear from Family

Meanwhile, Haitians in the diaspora are desperate to know what's going on. Have their family members all died?

"What did you hear, Zili?" those Haitians outside of Haiti say to me, Haitians whose $2 billion annual remittances to Haiti are crucial every year.

"Is all of Kafou really gone?" one asks. "My family lives there. My sister was going to have a baby. She just got her papers to come to the U.S. and be with us. Anything you hear, Zili? Please, are planes landing in Haiti yet? Can I take a boat there? I've got to go home. I want to see my sister."

We're trying to locate her sister. We're also trying to find out where our colleagues are in Haiti. Their families want to know if we know anything. Three of the schools we help are buried under shattered concrete. More than 800 children go there, and we don't know where they are, or their teachers. And I don't know where my friends are, or where all my family is, or whether they are safe.

Before five o'clock Tuesday, January 12, we were working at overcapacity, stretching to give voice to Haiti's pain and oppression. Shouting at Jericho walls for twenty years. Before we were ignored. Now they want us to tell them how we feel about 12,000 U.S. troops arriving. They want us to say how wonderful it is that the U.S. cares so much for the people of Haiti that it's giving us such priority. They want us to forget about

> The U.S. military is about domination and conquest, as Haitians know too well.

before January 12. Concentrate on now and how we all must come together now.

Mwen bouke—I am tired. I want to give them what they want. But I know better. Yesterday, I died again. We're buried alive under the concrete weight of the U.S./Euro narrative on Haiti. No one sees us. But we are Ayiti and we've died a living death too many times to take death seriously. We're traumatized, bruised, and bloodied. But we're still here because we can handle this and all that we know is still to come as we're "rescued" some more.

The U.S. Military Invasion Must Stop

I want the U.S. military invasion of Haiti to stop now. Soldiers are trained to kill, not provide humanitarian relief. And the U.S. military is about domination and conquest, as Haitians know too well.

We lived through a brutal U.S. military occupation from 1915 to 1934. We endured the U.S.-supported [Jean-Claude] Duvalier dictatorships that followed. We saw the hands of the U.S. government in the regime changes of 1991 and 2004 that forced President [Jean-Bertrand]Aristide from office.

The strong-arm tactics of the U.S. are on display again. Soldiers took over the airport the day after they arrived, over the objections of the Haitians working in the damaged control tower, who were pushed aside like trash.

The U.S. military is using the airport for important things, don't you see? Those buried under the rubble—hundreds of thousands of homeless Haitians who have not eaten or found clean water to drink when the mountains crumbled on them—can wait.

First, the Americans, Canadians, and Europeans who have been stuck in Haiti for two interminable days must be rescued immediately. Haitians, with nowhere to go, can wait.

The United States has blocked lifesaving first responders from landing, including Haitian doctors and nurses and other rescue teams. It is exploiting this disaster to direct Haiti's priorities and impose its own agenda.

Right now you need U.S. government clearance to land in Haiti. This is not independence. This is not self-rule.

Haitians are heartbroken and in unspeakable pain. But we are not idiots or under so much duress as to not object to the United States, Canada, and France speeding up their proxy U.N. occupation plans for taking Haitian lands and divvying up Haiti's oil, gold, iridium, and other mineral resources behind the veil of this emergency relief. The earthquake's depopulation of the coastal areas of Port-au-Prince may make that acquisition all the easier.

Haiti needs 12,000 doctors. Obama sent 12,000 troops to help us to death.

Haiti is not in conflict or at war with anyone. Haitians are not a violent people. In fact, there's more violence in Jamaica, the Dominican Republic, Brazil, Mexico, and Colombia than there is in Haiti.

And as much as the U.S media and the Pentagon wanted footage of U.S. soldiers rescuing Haitians, the people that could get saved got saved mostly by Haitians frantically using their bare hands to dig through the rubble and lift pulverized concrete in the immediate forty-eight hours after the earthquake. They did what they could to save themselves, as they have been doing since 1503 when the white settlers' "New World" began.

U.S. Troops Must Go Home

Go home, U.S. troops. Please. While at least 70,000 unidentified Haitians lie buried in mass graves and the count may top 200,000 killed, the people who could have been saved under the rubble and metal have died. Now it's about medical relief, healing, and rebuilding. Haitians can do that by themselves with the help of the world that

A US soldier sits in an armored vehicle in downtown Port-au-Prince. Some critics feared that the US military could become more than just a helpful presence in Haiti. (© AP Images/ Ramon Espinosa.)

wants to send monies to Haiti for the earthquake victims. We don't need the Pentagon.

Let the millions of Haitians in the diaspora take care of their own in solidarity with individuals of goodwill, from all the races and nations, who will work directly with the Haitian government and us, the people of Haiti.

Our time for change has come. Let's work together to help the earthquake victims, but with dignity and human rights and without the pain and menace of pointing military guns in shattered faces, weary souls.

There's an old Haitian proverb: "When you're playing with a wolf, you must expect to be scratched in the face."

We've been scratched too often. Our wounds are too raw right now. We can't play anymore with your wolves in sheep's clothing.

A frantic mother calls me from Haiti. "With my bare hands, I pulled my two daughters out from the rubble myself but I can't get them to a working hospital," she says. "I searched all night Tuesday to find them in the dark and under the concrete. My other two are dead. I don't have a way to fly to the Dominican Republic for care. The doctors say one crushed leg must be amputated but they don't have the equipment to do so. There are too many dead people at the hospital. I am carrying her somewhere else. I don't know where. There's no water or food to give them. I can't get inside the house to recover anything."

"I'll let your husband know you three are alive," I say. "Hang in there," I say. "Help is coming."

> Venezuelan and Cuban relief teams got [to Haiti] before the world's richest country and number one superpower.

The United States Prevents Families from Finding Loved Ones

Venezuelan and Cuban relief teams got there before the world's richest country and number one superpower. The United States, with a base next door to Haiti in Guantanamo Bay, Cuba, got there two days later, mostly after everyone had died under the rubble and baking in the hot tropical sun, trapped inside concrete and metal tombs that used to be homes, schools, or businesses.

Obama just stopped deportations, finally granting Temporary Protected Status to Haitian nationals in the United States, but his team said earthquake survivors in Haiti with nowhere to go won't be welcomed in America. Here's a letter we received:

> Zili, please help me bring my wife and my son here to the United States. My son is only fifteen months old. He was injured when a block fell on top his head. They both are homeless, with no medical care, no food, no shelter. My son, he is an American citizen. But the American Embassy requested a DNA test for him. The U.S. Embassy already granted a visa to my wife, but because of the DNA test she couldn't leave him alone. Please help me.

Haitians who flew on commercial planes toward Haiti and were waiting for the landing strip to open up for their planes to land were sent back.

"I want to see my sister," another said to me. "Why do the *Blan*—the foreigners—always have more important business to take care of in Haiti than me?"

Her plane was redirected to Miami, where she waits in agony. The moral support she wanted to give to whomever she found still alive at her house, the money she borrowed from families in Canada so she could bring something to whomever she found still alive, is not important.

"My wife is waiting for me," another said to me. "She knows I am coming. She knows I'm coming no matter what I have to do to get to her." His plane is redirected to the Dominican Republic. He says he's taking a bus into Cap-Haitien. He says he will walk if he has to, down to Port-au-Prince to find his wife.

"They're evacuating Port-au-Prince," I say.

He said, "Lightning may strike, thunder may fall and shatter me on the way there, but I swear to God they won't stop me from finding my family."

The next day, more than 7,000 Haitians were buried in a mass grave to clean up the streets. Are his two dead daughters in those graves with the rest of the unidentified dead? Did his wife manage to find a hospital to amputate the other's crushed leg? Even if the father from abroad walks to Port-au-Prince after crossing through the Dominican Republic, how hopeless and harrowing is his task? He may die over and over again, be left with no closure like so many of the millions of Haitians living abroad. They shall feel they've let down their families.

But never mind all that. The media wants me to stoke their feeding frenzy, begs me to talk to them about American missionaries who sacrifice all.

The US Military Is Welcome in Haiti

Mitchell Landsberg

In the following viewpoint, *Los Angeles Times* journalist Mitchell Landsberg describes the arrival of US troops in Haiti who came to provide humanitarian assistance after the devastating earthquake. He recites the history of US intervention in Haitian politics and US military occupation of Haiti. Given this history, he finds it surprising that most Haitians welcomed the US troops. In addition, he notes that the US soldiers found it satisfying to be able to help people.

Cite Soleil looks like a place where an American soldier might be expected to fight. An impossibly crowded warren of tin-roofed shacks, open sewers and blind alleys, it is one of the poorest slums in the Americas, with a long history of unrest, crime and violence.

So picture the scene: Just as dawn was breaking Sunday, a battle-hardened platoon from the Army's

---

SOURCE. Mitchell Landsberg, "In Haiti, US Troops Embrace a New Role," *Los Angeles Times*, January 25, 2010. Copyright © 2010. Los Angeles Times. Reprinted with permission.

82nd Airborne Division rolled into the area behind a well-armed convoy of Brazilian soldiers attached to the United Nations' longtime peacekeeping mission in Haiti.

Smoke from cooking and trash fires filled the air, reducing visibility in places to less than a city block but failing to cover the smell of rotting garbage and human waste. Pigs and feral dogs rooted through trash.

> "The U.S. military [is] providing much of the muscle behind getting aid into the country and out to the population."

It was an ominous setting for what turned out to be an entirely benign event. As soldiers traded fist bumps with children, good-natured adults formed orderly lines to receive the first major shipment of food aid to reach Cite Soleil, a neighborhood in Haiti's capital, since the Jan. 12 earthquake.

"Whatever they give us, we're satisfied," said Wilna Vertus, a 21-year-old mother of six, "because we don't have anything."

U.S. Troops Provide Aid

The U.S. military has been in Haiti since the day after the magnitude 7.0 quake, providing much of the muscle behind getting aid into the country and out to the population. For troops here, many of them veterans of combat in Iraq and Afghanistan, this is not the mission they trained for. Some critics have suggested that they are not getting enough aid to enough people fast enough.

Still, it has cast the troops in a gratifying, if somewhat unfamiliar, role as peaceful warriors who save lives rather than take them.

"It's kind of cool for a change," said Sgt. Eric DeJesus, a 26-year-old from New Jersey who was at the wheel of a Humvee as the convoy made its way into Cite Soleil. "I mean, we do this in Iraq, but at the same time there we're killing people, you know what I mean?"

There are now 3,700 U.S. troops in Haiti, plus at least 9,000 military personnel on ships just off the coast. So far, they have been involved almost entirely in aid deliveries, with very little work in security, which is mostly being handled by Haitian police and the U.N.'s 7,000-strong peacekeeping force.

Given the history of U.S. intervention in Haiti, which included a 20-year occupation in the early 20th century, Haitians might be expected to be resentful or fearful of a large contingent of U.S. soldiers and Marines. So far that does not seem to be the case.

US Army soldiers assist with food distribution in Cite Soleil, Haiti, two weeks after the earthquake. (© Chuck Liddy/MCT via Getty Images.)

The prevailing attitude was summed up by Saintalis Frisnel, a 37-year-old man with four children he can barely feed and cannot afford to educate. He was clutching a pair of liter bottles of water and half a dozen high-protein biscuits he had just received from American soldiers. It was not enough, he said. It could hardly feed his family for even a day. But he wasn't complaining.

"They're doing good for me," he said of the Americans. "If it was my government, I could never get a chance to touch one of these crackers."

Cite Soleil, which has a population estimated between 400,000 and 500,000, escaped the worst of the quake's destruction, perhaps because there is so much less to destroy than in more affluent parts of Port-au-Prince. The best houses in the area, which is wedged between the city's harbor and airport, are concrete bunkers with tin roofs, perhaps 100 square feet in all. Most show little or no sign of damage. Frisnel said his house, made almost entirely of corrugated tin, fell down, but no one was seriously hurt.

As is the case for many of Haiti's poorest citizens, his house was too flimsy to kill anyone.

A Place Where Suffering Is the Norm

Still, suffering is the norm in Cite Soleil, and the earthquake has only made things worse. What little work people had is mostly gone. It is harder for them to replace whatever they have lost, because they have so little to begin with.

Befitting the community's status as Haiti's largest slum, Sunday's aid delivery was overseen by the commanding generals of U.S. and U.N. forces in Haiti.

At a news conference on a blocked-off road, Army Lt. Gen. P.K. Keen, the U.S. commander, defended the military against accusations that it was moving too slowly, although he acknowledged that much more needed to be done.

Keen said that far more people in the capital need food assistance than are being reached. However, neither Keen nor his U.N. counterpart, Brazilian Gen. Floriano Peixoto, could say how many people were being helped so far.

"The aid . . . is being pushed out," Keen said. "But again, the need is tremendous. Every day is a better day than yesterday, and tomorrow will be a better day than today."

Keen said he didn't know how long American forces would be needed in Haiti, but added, "I think it would be a tragedy—a tragedy—to not have sufficient forces to feed the people."

Keen said it made sense for the U.S. military to play a leading role in providing assistance after a disaster whose death toll has not been calculated, though the Haitian government said Sunday that more than 150,000 bodies had been buried so far by a company hired to collect corpses.

A New Experience for Troops

Keen's soldiers seemed to agree with him, although they said it was not the most natural role for them to play.

"We've got a lot of combat veterans who deployed to Iraq or Afghanistan," said 1st Lt. Jay Rosen of Union Bridge, Md. "For them, this is a whole new experience."

That was not entirely true for Sgt. 1st Class Chad Lewis, who had been to Haiti before on a humanitarian mission. But he has also had more than his share of combat deployments, including stints in Iraq and Kosovo. And when he arrived in Haiti, he said, he was loaded up with ammunition and prepared for the worst.

Since then, he's been thinking of taking off his protective gear "and walking around like everybody else."

"Part of me loves the combat job," he said, "because that's what I do. . . . But I'm also a softy. I think anybody with a heart would want to be here helping."

Nursing Mothers Donate Breast Milk for Haitian Infants

Tamara Lytle

In the following viewpoint, Tamara Lytle reports on the donation of breast milk by nursing mothers in the United States who wanted to help infants in Haiti. Getting the milk to Haiti, however, proved to be a difficult task, because it required commercial plane flights and helicopters. The milk eventually landed on the USNS *Comfort* hospital ship and then was stored in the ship's freezers. Although many mothers wanted to donate more milk, keeping the milk frozen and finding adequate freezer space was a big obstacle to the effort. Lytle is a journalist who writes for *U.S. News & World* Report and AOL News.

SOURCE. Tamara Lytle, "Tiny Bottles of Relief Arrive for Haiti's Newborns," AOL News, January 28, 2010. aolnews.com. Content © 2012 AOL Inc. AOL and the AOL logo are trademarks of AOL Inc. Used with permission.

For newborns struggling for life in the aftermath of Haiti's earthquake, 140 tiny but powerful bottles of relief arrived Thursday [January 27, 2010] afternoon: breast milk donated by American mothers.

The bottles were no bigger than travel toiletries—3 ounces—but chock full of the nutrients and immunities so vital to babies. Especially babies suffering from injuries and illness or born prematurely in a disaster area.

When a U.S. Navy helicopter carrying the precious cargo touched down on the USNS *Comfort* hospital ship, which sits off the coast of the devastated country, it was the final leg of a complicated sprint.

Red Tape Nearly Scuttles Donation

But after surviving a commercial plane flight, a charter ride, a helicopter trip and two days on dry ice, the milk ran headlong into red tape.

Navy spokesman Lt. David Shark, who is aboard the *Comfort*, said U.S. Office of Foreign Disaster Assistance [OFDA], which is part of USAID [United States Agency for International Development], complained about the idea of distributing donated breast milk and issued a statement calling it an "unfeasible and unsafe intervention."

"We acknowledge the generosity of the donor of the breast milk but have concerns based on years of best practices. It is the humanitarian community's position that supporting donations of donor breast milk is not recommended in emergencies for a number of reasons," the OFDA statement said.

"These reasons include huge logistical constraints, lack of cold chain supply, and no clear guidance on ethical issues, breast milk screening, and continuity of supply," it said.

The Milk Makes It to a Freezer

But Shark said the milk may still be used. The important "cold chain" was preserved—meaning the milk stayed

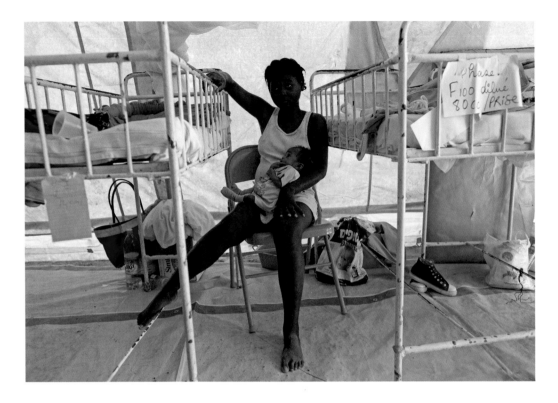

At the General Hospital in Port-au-Prince, Haiti, Farah Paul holds her malnourished baby, who stopped breast-feeding the day after the earthquake. (© AP Images/Rodrigo Abd.)

frozen during the trip. Doctors from the *Comfort*, which has more than 200 military medical personnel aboard, will make a presentation to the task force that oversees U.S. efforts in Haiti.

"There [is] a very real possibility we will be using the product soon," Shark said. Meanwhile, the milk sits in two Styrofoam coolers just inside a large freezer on the *Comfort*.

The effort to get that milk into the *Comfort*'s freezer began on Tuesday, as word went out to mothers' groups around the country that the Haitian babies needed help. The nation's 10 nonprofit milk banks—which usually get breast milk donations for medically fragile American infants whose mothers cannot provide it—were quickly flooded with hundreds of calls from mothers touched by the images of devastation in Haiti since the 7.0-magnitude earthquake hit Jan. 12.

"It shows the best of the best the U.S. can muster," said Pauline Sakamoto, head of the Human Milk Banking Association of North America, which provided the milk. "It's just an outpouring of support."

All those offers of donations will help any future shipments to Haiti if there are any and replenish the already low supplies in U.S. milk banks. The first shipment was culled from supplies on hand and handed off Tuesday morning to Quick International Courier, which donated its services to get the milk to Haiti and handled all the complications involved in keeping the milk frozen.

> By [January 27] the milk was aboard and ready for premature babies and other sick infants.

The frozen milk arrived in the wee hours of Thursday morning in Port-au-Prince and was picked up by a Navy helicopter. By Thursday afternoon the milk was aboard and ready for premature babies and other sick infants, some of them orphaned by the disaster.

Donors Hope to Send More Milk

Amanda Nickerson, head of the International Breast Milk Project, which led the effort, said 1,000 ounces were ready to ship. But the *Comfort* didn't have enough freezer space. Her nonprofit had made a similar shipment to the Philippines last October after a typhoon and regularly sends milk to infants in South Africa, many of them orphaned by AIDS. She hopes to send more milk to Haiti.

Haiti has 37,000 pregnant women in its capital alone, and 10,000 of them are due in the next 30 days, according to Alina Labrada of CARE, a nonprofit that fights poverty and helps women and children around the world. Conditions there are still difficult, said Labrada, whose organization has 30 workers in the country. "The water is so dirty, the sanitation is such a problem, a lot of women don't have enough to eat and drink themselves and aren't going to make enough milk."

Sakamoto said she hopes Americans also will donate to organizations that help Haitian mothers breast-feed amid the chaotic aftermath of the earthquake.

The dirty water in Haiti also means that formula can be dangerous for babies in displaced families who don't have clean water to mix with it.

The International Lactation Consultant Association on Thursday warned people not to send formula to Haiti. After the Asian tsunamis, formula donations caused a tripling of diarrheal disease, according to the association.

The Process of Milk Donation

U.S. milk banks regularly take donations from mothers after putting the donors through a screening test similar to what's done for blood donations. The women also must take a blood test and get approval from their doctors. The milk comes from mothers who are pumping milk for their own children and end up with extra. The milk is pasteurized and frozen.

In 2008—the most recent year for which figures are available—Sakamoto's organization shipped 1.4 million ounces of milk out to neonatal intensive care units and other doctors to dispense.

Dane Nutty, outreach director of the Indiana Mothers' Milk Bank, said he hopes to find a way to help Haitian infants who aren't on the *Comfort*. The logistics are daunting.

"If you have a country without power, how are you going to store the milk?" Nutty asked. "We are building up our supplies so that when we do work out the logistics on land, we will have a supply ready."

Meanwhile, the new donors could help shore up supplies for U.S. babies.

"This is a phenomenal response," Sakamoto said. "But there are kids in this country in the same situation that need this milk. They may not be in a major earthquake, but they can't tolerate other food sources and they have high-risk medical [conditions]."

International Health Organizations Call for Appropriate Infant Feeding in Haiti

UNICEF, WHO, and WFP

The following viewpoint is taken from a joint statement issued by the United Nations Children's Fund (UNICEF), the World Health Organization (WHO), and the World Food Programme (WFP) concerning the importance of breast-feeding in emergency situations. The organizations call for all aid organizations to protect and support breast-feeding as it is the best way to avoid infant illness and death. They further discourage the use of breast-milk substitutes because of the potential for contamination. Finally, they call for reintroducing breast-feeding to bottle-fed children.

During emergency situations, disease and death rates among under-five children are higher than for any other age group; the younger the infant the higher the risk. Mortality risk is particularly high because of the combined impact of a greatly increased prevalence of communicable diseases and diarrhoea and soaring rates of under-nutrition. *Appropriate feeding and care of infants and young children is essential to preventing malnutrition, morbidity and mortality.*

Breastfeeding Is a Lifeline During the Crisis

Major health problems among Haitian children, which have been exacerbated by this crisis, are acute and chronic malnutrition and communicable diseases. Given the structural damage caused by the earthquake to water supply systems, there is an additional risk of water borne diseases affecting large numbers of the urban, rural and displaced populations. Many infants and young children have been orphaned or separated from their mothers. Risks to children in Haiti are exacerbated by pre-earthquake poor infant and young child feeding practices and malnutrition. In this emergency situation, the lifeline offered by exclusive breastfeeding to children for the first six months of life and continued breastfeeding with complementary feeding for two years or more is of utmost importance and must be protected, promoted and supported as much as possible.

Most mothers initiate breastfeeding in Haiti, and the majority of infants less than six months of age were at least partially breastfed prior to the earthquake. At this stage it is critical to encourage and support mothers to initiate breastfeeding immediately after the delivery, exclusively breastfeed up to six months and for those with infants below six months who 'mix feed' to revert to exclusive breastfeeding. Non-breastfed infants are at especially high risk and need early identification and targeted

skilled support, including re-establishing breastfeeding (relactation).

Protection and support for breastfeeding women. No food or liquid other than breast milk, not even water, is needed to meet an infant's nutritional and fluid requirements during the first six months of life. The valuable protection from infection that breastfeeding confers is all the more important in environments without safe water supply and sanitation. Therefore, creation of a protective environment and provision of skilled support to breastfeeding women are essential interventions. There is a common misconception that in emergencies, many mothers can no longer breastfeed adequately because of stress or inadequate nutrition. Concern for these mothers and their infants can fuel donations of breastmilk substitutes (BMS) such as infant formula. Although stress can temporarily interfere with the flow of breastmilk, it

A Red Cross worker holds a baby suffering from severe dehydration following the earthquake. Logistics for getting milk to infants proved to be difficult for aid workers. (© Chris Hondros/Getty Images.)

is not likely to inhibit breastmilk production, provided mothers and infants remain together and are supported to initiate and continue breastfeeding. Mothers who lack food or who are malnourished can still breastfeed. Provision of adequate fluids and food for mothers must be a priority as it will help to protect their health and well-being as well as that of their young children.

Basic interventions to facilitate breastfeeding include prioritising mothers with young children for shelter, food, security, and water and sanitation, enabling mother-to-mother support, providing specific space for skilled breastfeeding counselling and support to maintain or re-establish lactation. Traumatised and depressed mothers may have difficulty responding to their infants and require particular mental and emotional support. UNICEF [United Nations Children's Fund], WHO [World Health Organization] and other organizations involved in infant feeding in emergencies will support training of staff on individual assessment of the best options for feeding infants, as well as education and support of caregivers on optimal infant feeding in these emergency circumstances.

> Artificial feeding in an emergency . . . is a last resort [used] only when other safer options have first been fully explored.

Feeding of the non-breastfed child less than six months of age.

Infants less than six months of age who are not breastfed need urgent identification and targeted skilled support. The priority to feed these infants should be relactation. If this is not possible or when artificial feeding is indicated by skilled staff such as health providers or infant feeding counsellors, breast-milk substitutes are necessary and must be accompanied by training on hygiene, preparation and use to minimise their associated risks. Artificial feeding in an emergency carries high risks of malnutrition, illness and death and is a last resort only when other safer options have first been fully explored. . . .

When breast-milk substitutes are used caregivers should be encouraged and taught to feed with a cup and spoon. Bottles and teats should not be provided as they are more difficult to clean. Skilled support by appropriately trained staff should be provided to caregivers on how to use the breast-milk substitute safely. Because infants receiving breast-milk substitutes are at increased risk for illness, a mechanism to monitor their health should be established.

Donations of Infant Formula Should Not Be Made

Donations and procurement of breast-milk substitutes and other milk products.
In accordance with internationally accepted guidelines, donations of infant formula, bottles and teats and other powdered or liquid milk and milk products should not be made. Experience with past emergencies has shown an excessive quantity of products, which are poorly targeted, endangering infants' lives. Any *procurement* of breast milk substitutes should be based on careful needs assessment and in coordination with UNICEF. Human milk donations while safe when processed and pasteurized in a human milk bank also require fully functioning cold chains. Such conditions are not currently met in Haiti and human milk donations cannot be used at present. All queries and any donations that do appear should be directed to UNICEF, the designated nutrition coordinating agency in Haiti.

Complementary feeding of children above six months of age.
Children from the age of six months require nutrient-rich, age-appropriate and safe complementary foods in

addition to breast milk. Priority should be placed on locally available, culturally acceptable, nutritionally adequate and age-appropriate foods. When cooking facilities are nonexistent or severely limited, ready-to-use fortified foods are an option. Micronutrient powders that can be added to local foods, emergency rations or blended foods will also improve dietary quality. In addition, once cooking facilities have been set up, provision of fortified blended food is recommended. A monitoring system to ensure the appropriate targeting, distribution and use of food and food products for infants and young children should be established. . . .

UNICEF, WHO and WFP [World Food Programme] strongly urge all who are involved in funding, planning and implementing the emergency response in Haiti to avoid unnecessary illness and death by promoting, protecting and supporting breastfeeding and appropriate complementary feeding and by preventing uncontrolled distribution and use of breast-milk substitutes. Public and private sector entities and individuals who wish to support infants and young children and their mothers and caregivers in this emergency should donate funds rather than send goods. We further urge governments and partners to include capacity building for breastfeeding and infant and young child feeding as part of emergency preparedness and planning, and to commit financial and human resources for appropriate and timely protection, promotion and support of optimal infant and young child feeding in this and other emergencies.

A Christian Group Illegally Takes Haitian Children

Matthew Clark

In the following viewpoint, journalist Matthew Clark reports on the arrest of ten members of a Baptist charity who tried to take a group of children out of Haiti after the earthquake and into the Dominican Republic without authorization. The group argued they were merely trying to provide a better life for the children and thus had done nothing wrong. The Haitian government, however, viewed the situation as child trafficking, particularly when it appeared that many of the children were not orphans at all. Clark reviews a similarly misguided situation that took place in Chad in 2007 that endangered legitimate aid workers. Clark is the Latin American editor for the *Christian Science Monitor*.

SOURCE. Matthew Clark, "Haiti 'Orphan' Rescue Mission: Adoption or Child Trafficking?," *Christian Science Monitor*, February 1, 2010. Reproduced by permission from Christian Science Monitor (www .csmonitor.com).

When does adoption become child trafficking? That question seems to be the last thing that Haiti's notoriously ill-equipped, underfunded, and understaffed government needs to be tackling in the wake of the Jan. 12 earthquake that leveled the capital, Port-au-Prince. But Saturday's [January 30, 2010] arrest of 10 members of an Idaho-based Baptist charity for trying to take 33 Haitian children across the border with the Dominican Republic without proper paperwork has become an international incident. And it now threatens to be a serious distraction from the daunting task of providing food, shelter, and security for the more than 1 million left homeless by the quake.

The members of the New Life Children's Refuge said that they were only trying to provide a better life for the children and denied that the group had done anything wrong. But the problem with following their highest sense of right without proper permission from the authorities is that it may technically be child trafficking. And in a weak country where that illicit trade has exploded in recent years, the authorities are taking this quite seriously.

> The New Life members had no government-issued paperwork of any kind as they attempted to take the children across the border.

Prime Minister Max Bellerive denounced the group's "illegal trafficking of children."

"This is an abduction, not an adoption," said Social Affairs Minister Yves Christallin, explaining that children need authorization from the ministry to leave the country.

Apparently, the New Life members had no government-issued paperwork of any kind as they attempted to take the children across the border. "When asked about the children's documents, they had no documents," Haitian Culture and Communications Minister Marie Laurence Jocelyn Lassegue said.

Amid intense media interest, Laura Silsby of the New Life Children's Refuge organization enters a court building in Haiti after being arrested for the alleged trafficking of Haitian children. (© AP Images/ Javier Galeano.)

"You can't just go and take a child out of a country— no matter what country you are in," said Kent Page, a spokesman for UNICEF in Haiti. "There are processes that have to be followed. You can't just pick up a child and walk out of a country with a child, no matter what your best intentions are."

Determining the Right Thing to Do

Group leader Laura Silsby said they paid no money for the children and that the group had documents from the Dominican government but did not seek paperwork from Haitian authorities. "In this chaos the government is in right now, we were just trying to do the right thing," said Ms. Silsby.

But what is the right thing to do? Smart, earnest people agree to disagree.

As the *Monitor* reported last week, the increased US demand for adopting Haitian children in the wake of the earthquake is "churning up the advocates of streamlined adoption procedures for Haiti against those who say too-hasty adoption can hurt the children and birthparents that in some cases still exist."

It's tempting to want to airlift children out of Haiti, getting them out of harm's way immediately," says Michelle Brané, director of [the New York-based Women's Refugee Commission's] detention and asylum program. "But it's important to remember that in the current chaos, thousands of people, including parents and children, are still searching for their families. Removing children from countries too quickly after an emergency," she adds, can "jeopardize family reunification efforts . . . and increase the risk that children will fall into the hands of traffickers and other ill-intentioned individuals.

> It began to emerge that many of the children were not even orphans.

Not Orphans?

The purpose of New Life's "Haitian Orphan Rescue Mission" was to "rescue Haitian orphans abandoned on the streets, makeshift hospitals or from collapsed orphanages in Port-au-Prince and surrounding areas, and bring them to New Life Children's Refuge in Cabarete, Dominican Republic."

Child Trafficking Increases Dramatically After the Earthquake

The [Haiti] earthquake created a mass exodus which makes it hard at times to differentiate between smugglers and parents or relatives crossing the border with children. Some of these minors are now offering their sexual services to affluent foreigners in tourist resorts on the western part of the Island. A zero-tolerance policy against traffickers has to be effectively implemented so as to stop thousands of children becoming victims of their crimes and bring them to justice.

SOURCE. *Daniel Ruiz, "Restavèks and Child Trafficking in Haiti,"* Freedom from Fear, Issue 8, December 2011. *Freedomfromfearmagazine.org.*

But on Sunday it began to emerge that many of the children were not even orphans, reports Agence France-Presse.

"The majority of these children have families. Some of the older ones said their parents are alive, and some gave an address and phone numbers," said Patricia Vargas, the regional director of the Austria-based orphan charity SOS Children, which is now looking after the 33 children at its orphanage on the outskirts of Port-au-Prince.

An Earlier Orphan Debacle

The whole episode in Haiti is reminiscent of another orphan debacle in the African nation of Chad that the *Monitor* reported on in 2007. Back then, 16 Europeans from a France-based group called Zoe's Ark were charged with trying to smuggle 103 children out of eastern Chad in what the charity workers said was an attempt to save orphans affected by the conflict across the border in Sudan's Darfur region.

The group tried to circumvent Chadian authorities and fly the children out of the country on a chartered plane. But after it emerged that many of the children were not orphans or from Darfur, locals in Abéché, Chad, began protesting angrily outside the group's local offices. Western aid groups in the area began to fear for their safety as mistrust of foreigners began to swirl.

A few months later, six French members of Zoe's Ark were convicted of attempting to kidnap the 103 children and sentenced to eight years of hard labor and ordered to pay restitution amounting to close to $9 million.

Chad's president, Idriss Deby—a longtime beneficiary of French military and financial support—eventually pardoned the group and they were returned to France.

But not before significant damage had been done, as the *Monitor* reported.

> In sub-Saharan Africa, the case played powerfully as an instance of white colonial arrogance; in France, it was seen as a misguided effort to save lives; and among humanitarian groups it has been seen as the kind of mission that puts experienced, professional aid workers at risk.

Awaiting a Decision

Back in Haiti, Justice Secretary Amarick Louis said a commission would meet today to determine whether the New Life group would go before a judge.[1]

Meanwhile, the group is praying for a little leniency.

"We are trusting the truth will be revealed and we are praying for that," said Silsby.

Back in Idaho at the Central Valley Baptist Church where five of the 10 arrested workers attend services, the Rev. Clint Henry told CNN that the whole community is disturbed by the events, but praying for understanding.

Said Mr. Henry: "We are praying that the motive and intent will be clearly understood in the courts down there."

Note

1. A judge dropped the kidnapping charges in April 2010. Group leader Laura Silsby was held on illegal travel charges and released in May 2010.

Christians Are Urged to Adopt Haitian Children Orphaned by the Earthquake

Christianity Today

In the following viewpoint, the editors of *Christianity Today*, a US Christian magazine founded by evangelist Billy Graham, argue that Christian leaders and churches ought to advocate for the reform of international adoption, making it easier for US Christians to adopt children from overseas. They believe that requiring a child to live a deprived life in the child's home country is not in the child's best interest. They also note the biblical injunction that Christians should take care of widows and orphans.

Two years ago, a Christian couple from Chambersburg, Pennsylvania, fell in love with an abandoned toddler, born with a disability and living in an orphanage in rural Haiti. Already adoptive parents of a Liberian child, Katy and Josh Manges decided to adopt the toddler, Malachi, who has a treatable bone disorder.

Then the January 12 [2010] earthquake that crushed so much of Port-au-Prince, costing an estimated 230,000 lives, put the prayerful plans of the Manges family in limbo. It also laid bare before the world how badly orphans and vulnerable children may be treated when they get caught up in red tape, corruption, and political correctness.

For the Manges family, the outcome was success. In late February, Malachi arrived in Miami into the welcoming arms of his new family. Yet the adoption required two years of effort, delayed by local politics and requiring a personal signature from Haiti's prime minister. At the last minute, rioters at Port-au-Prince's airport derailed Malachi's departure, falsely alleging that he and other adoptees had phony paperwork.

Adoptive Parents Are Needed

This episode stands alongside another, the still-unfolding saga of the Idaho Baptists who were arrested on suspect charges of child trafficking. The latter may have a long-lasting chilling effect on inter-country adoption just when adoptive parents are needed more than ever. There are 210 million orphans worldwide, and adoptions to the U.S. have dropped 45 percent since 2004.

The greater problem isn't with potential adopting parents. It's with a system that is severely broken. Christian leaders and churches have much to offer in advocating for the reform of confusing adoption laws, stronger enforcement of international norms, and making adoption more affordable, more visible, and a more honored practice.

Katy Manges (left) and her husband, Josh, adopted Malachi (center) in 2010. The earthquake and allegations of child trafficking in Haiti caused delays in the Mangeses being united with their new son. (© AP Images/ Lynne Sladky.)

Haiti's Children Have Many Needs

Jedd Medefind, president of the Christian Alliance for Orphans, recently told *Christianity Today* that immediately after Haiti's quake, many agencies fielded waves of calls from people with a strong impulse to take Haitian orphans into their homes. Rather than dismiss or belittle this impulse, Medefind encouraged them to consider the many ways of supporting the children, recognizing that adoption is a long and uncertain process. Family reunification, orphanages, extended family care, and child sponsorship all have a role to play in meeting the needs of vulnerable children in crisis or chronic need.

But Medefind is quick to note that powerful political and cultural barriers often make adoption an arduous process that takes too long and costs too much. "The reality is that there are thousands of children, before and after the earthquake, who are genuinely in need of parents," he says. "To the extent that parents can't be found, we should not relegate children to living on the streets or [in] orphanages. The political and cultural factors often become unspoken reasons why children are forced to remain in institutional care or on the streets, which is a profound tragedy."

> It isn't in the best interest of abandoned children to grow up destitute and barely literate, regardless of the imagined cultural benefit of remaining in their home country.

Adoption Is in the Best Interest of Many Haitian Children

The political and cultural barriers stem from warped ideas about what is in a poor child's best interest. It isn't in the best interest of abandoned children to grow up destitute and barely literate, regardless of the imagined cultural benefit of remaining in their home country. Haiti itself is a vivid example of injustice. The government tolerates a modern form of child slavery by allowing 225,000 children ages 6–14 to work as *restavecs* (unpaid, indentured domestics).

Adoption, domestic or inter-country, should not be looked down upon as inferior at best or as a last resort. The 150,000 South Korean orphans adopted worldwide (99,000 to the U.S.) since the 1950s testify well to the durable difference a loving adoptive family can make.

Christians Should Adopt

For Christians, the biblical basis for adoption bears repeating. The Book of James beckons every true follower of Christ to become involved in the lives of orphans (and widows). It's not for married couples only. Godly, never-married singles have successfully adopted, and most readily affirm the ideal that each child should live with a mother and father—whenever possible. So, Christian singles should not be automatically excluded from the pool of possibilities for adoption.

Adoption experts provided *CT* [*Christianity Today*] with four ways churches can increase their involvement:

- give adoptive families space to tell their stories in church;
- find ways to give small starter grants to people interested in adopting;
- encourage the adoption of children with special needs; and
- develop a full spectrum of responses, from child sponsorship to adoption.

CT recently talked with a never-married woman who adopted a young girl from Kazakhstan into her home (at a personal initial cost of $36,000). For her, the question was, "Are we talking about live souls?" Not mere "victims" or "political symbols" or "the needy," but children for whom Christ died, who need a home where the love of God is lived and shared with the least of these.

Guidelines Are Established to Prevent the Illegal Adoption of Haitian Children After the Earthquake

Annie E. Casey Foundation

In the following viewpoint, representatives of the Annie E. Casey Foundation detail guidelines and resources for welfare organizations assisting Haitian families in the United States and in Haiti. The earthquake separated many children from their families; some of these children are orphans, but others need to be reunited with their birth families, not permanently adopted. The guidelines offered by the foundation seek to prevent illegal adoptions and

SOURCE. "After the Earthquake: A Bulletin for Child Welfare Organizations Assisting Haitian Families in the United States," Annie E. Casey Foundation, July 16, 2010. aecf.org. Copyright © 2010 by Annie E. Casey Foundation. All rights reserved. Reproduced by permission.

child trafficking. The Annie E. Casey Foundation is a private, charitable organization dedicated to improving the lives of children.

On January 12, 2010, a massive earthquake in Haiti caused a shocking loss of lives and millions of dollars in infrastructure damages. In the days following the earthquake, thousands of Haitians departed Haiti bound for North America, as well as nations such as France and the Netherlands. The United States, home to the largest concentration of Haitians in any country outside of Haiti, faces significant challenges, both immediate and long-term, as a result of this tragedy.

Demographic Background

The United States is home to approximately 785,676 persons reported to be of Haitian ancestry. Nearly 70 percent of the Haitian-born population resides in Florida and New York State.

The top five U.S. counties with Haitian populations are Miami-Dade, Florida, with 118,554 Haitian-born persons; Broward County, Florida, with 102,500; Kings County, New York, with 86,687; Palm Beach County, Florida, with 59,463; and Queens County, New York, with 42,064.

The Migration and Policy Institute reports:

- More than 25 percent of all foreign-born Haitians in the United States arrived in 2000 or later.

- Haitian immigrants are more likely than other immigrant groups to be naturalized United States citizens (48.4 percent compared to 43 percent among the overall foreign-born population).

- Approximately half of all Haitian immigrants have limited English proficiency.

- Nearly half of all U.S. adults born in Haiti have some college education.
- Nearly half of all employed Haitian-born men in the United States work in the service sector, or in construction, extraction, and transportation.
- More than one in every four employed Haitian-born immigrant women work in healthcare support.
- Haitian immigrants are less likely to live in poverty than other immigrant groups (12.9 percent lived below the poverty line in 2008 versus 14.9 percent of all foreign-born families).

The most recently published estimates from the U.S. Department of Homeland Security (DHS), based on an analysis of the 2000 Census, suggest that the unauthorized immigrant population from Haiti grew from 67,000 in 1990 to 76,000 in 2000. These estimates do not consider increased migration during the past decade or since the earthquake.

The Earthquake Hits Home

A *New York Times* survey from February 2010 found 59 percent of Haitian Americans lost a loved one in the earthquake. Since the tragedy, there have been reports of a continuous exodus of Haitians traveling to the Dominican Republic, arriving in the United States using a B-2 Tourist Visa (which covers short leisure or tourism visits), and staying with relatives and friends in communities such as Brooklyn and Miami.

In the wake of Haiti's devastation and its decimated infrastructure, DHS announced a temporary stay on deportations to Haiti in January 2010. While efforts to remove Haitians from the country slowed, the focus on keeping Haitians from entering America intensified. The U.S. Coast Guard, for example, has increased patrols in the Caribbean to deter illegal immigration and has returned a number of boats containing Haitians. . . .

The Children of Haiti, Then and Now

Even before the earthquake, Haiti suffered massive, systemic, and deep poverty. According to the World Bank, more than half of the population lived in extreme poverty, surviving on less than $1 a day. The United Nations had designated Haiti as one of the 50 "least developed countries" in the world. The Inter-American Development Bank considered the 2010 earthquake to be the most destructive natural disaster in modern times considering the size of Haiti's population and economy. Prior to the earthquake, as many as 380,000 children were estimated to be living in orphanages within the country. In the post-earthquake devastation, the number of orphans in Haiti has risen dramatically. In contrast to the United States, the terms "orphans" and "orphanages" in Haiti refer to both true orphans (those lacking parents) and to children whose parents' whereabouts are unknown or whose parents' poverty meant they could not support their children.

> In the post-earthquake devastation, the number of orphans in Haiti has risen dramatically.

In addition, pre-earthquake Haiti had a serious child trafficking problem, with numerous abandoned and homeless children living on the street. It also has a tradition of children living as household servants, many in slave-like conditions, called "restavek," a French word for "one who stays."

Following the earthquake, several steps have been taken to safeguard children, both those who are separated from their families and those whose families have died or are missing as a result of the disaster. The Haitian government, UNICEF, and international aid organizations have developed children's "safe zones" and a

Haitian children orphaned by the earthquake arrive in Miami, Florida, to be united with their new parents in late January 2010. (© Miami Herald/ MCT via Getty Images.)

registration system for unaccompanied children meant to reunify lost children and their families.

Principles Regarding Children Separated from Family

Organizations with experience handling large-scale disasters such as the Haiti earthquake have developed principles for coping with children separated from their parents and families as the result of a crisis. These children are considered a vulnerable population whose basic survival is in question and who face heightened risk of abuse and exploitation.

The *Guidelines for the Alternative Care of Children*, the first international document on caring for children without parents in non-emergency and emergency situations, was adopted by the United Nations General Assembly only a few months prior to the earthquake in Haiti. It underscores that in emergency situations, such as an earthquake, the primary goal is to track down and reunify children with their families to the maximum extent possible, prior to any other permanent solution being pursued. The principles of the *Guidelines* include:

- a registry of unaccompanied and separated children;
- temporary and long-term family-based care;
- rules that specify the use of residential care as a temporary measure only; and
- a prohibition on using large-scale residential facilities as permanent or long-term care solutions.

Many international child welfare organizations, such as International Social Service, Save the Children, SOS Children's Village International, and World Vision, have called for countries to adhere to the principles of the *Guidelines for the Alternative Care of Children*, as well as the Better Care Network's *Interagency Guiding Principles on Unaccompanied and Separated Children*.

Children Should Be Reunited with Their Families

In particular, these organizations stress the need to reunite children separated from their families rather than adopting them out of the country. These relief agencies also have called for an immediate moratorium on any new adoptions of children found on their own following the earthquake until exhaustive family tracing and reunification has been completed. The fear is that any hasty new adoptions would risk permanently breaking up families, causing long-term damage to already vulnerable children, and distract from aid efforts in Haiti. These organizations, however, have encouraged adoptions interrupted by the

> The fear is that any hasty new adoptions would risk permanently breaking up families, causing long-term damage to already vulnerable children.

disaster to move forward, as long as the appropriate legal documentation was in place prior to the earthquake and the adoptions meet Haitian, U.S., and international laws. . . .

The Policy for Orphans and Adoptees

On January 18, 2010, DHS, in coordination with the U.S. Department of State (DOS), announced a humanitarian parole policy allowing certain "orphan" children from Haiti to enter the United States temporarily on an individual basis. The departments are working together and have issued travel documents (either immigrant visas or humanitarian parole authorizations) for children who are cleared to travel so they may be united with their American adoptive parents.

Under applicable laws, unaccompanied minors entering the country without a parent or legal guardian are subject to special procedures regarding their custody and care. DHS coordinates with the Department of Health and Human Services' Office of Refugee Resettlement in the cases of these unaccompanied minors. All cases will be evaluated by U.S. Citizenship and Immigration Services (USCIS). Depending on their circumstances and information available, some children will receive immigrant visas with permanent immigration status and will require no further processing. Those who enter under humanitarian parole status will need to have their immigration status resolved after arrival.

At the request of the Haitian government, USCIS stopped accepting new requests for parole under the Special Humanitarian Parole Program for Haitian Orphans effective April 14, 2010. . . .

Conclusion

In times of natural disaster, children's needs for shelter, basic resources and family connections escalate dramatically. "The earthquake wreaked havoc, leaving countless children traumatized and either orphaned or separated from parents and relatives," says Annie E. Casey Foundation President and CEO Patrick T. McCarthy. In the midst of crucial efforts to provide food, shelter, and water in Haiti, there is a concurrent need in the United States to help Haitian children, families and communities as they face complex issues of disconnection and dislocation. "It is our hope that this bulletin, with its up-to-date information, provides the technical help to public systems, advocates and service providers who are addressing the pressing needs of Haitian youth and families in the United States," says McCarthy.

A US Evangelist Blames Haiti's Earthquake on Haitian Religion

Russell Goldman

In the following viewpoint, ABC news journalist Russell Goldman reports on statements by television evangelist Pat Robertson that the Haiti earthquake was directly connected to the Haitian people's belief in voodoo. Although most Haitians are Catholic, many also practice voodoo, especially in times of natural disaster. Robertson claims that many years ago, the Haitians swore a pact with the devil that they would serve the devil if he got rid of the French colonists. As a result, some religious leaders such as Robertson believe the country is cursed.

Where once they gathered in ornate cathedrals and vibrant voodoo temples, Port-au-Prince residents gathered Wednesday night in the streets to pray, their mournful supplications punctuated by the cries of survivors still trapped under the rubble of Tuesday's earthquake.

The hymns they sang were Christian, but religion in Haiti has long been a fluid mix of Catholic and Afro-Caribbean spiritual traditions, which for centuries have made the island country a battleground for Western missionaries who view voodoo as devil worship.

Christian Hostility to Voodoo

When American televangelist Pat Robertson on Wednesday [January 14, 2010] attributed the earthquake to the Haitian people's "pact to the devil," it shined a light on the hostility some foreign Christians have aimed at the country's religious traditions.

Some 80 percent of Haitians are practicing Roman Catholics. But despite their Christian faith, half the country's population practices voodoo, an Afro-Caribbean faith in which practitioners cast spells, conduct sacrifices, worship spirits and believe in zombies, according to statistics compiled by the *CIA World Factbook*.

Increasingly, evangelical Protestant faiths, like Pentecostalism, which stress a locally popular belief in an "unseen spirit world," have taken hold.

The earthquake killed Joseph Mio, archbishop of Port-au-Prince as well as some 100 Catholic priests, or about one in eight, and left an unknown number of priests, nuns and seminarians homeless. Catholic institutions, including the archbishop's palace and the city's primary cathedral in Port-au-Prince, were destroyed, as were countless voodoo temples, which served as important social-service institutions.

With many centerpieces of religious life destroyed, the effects the earthquake will have on the spiritual

landscape remain to be seen, according to Elizabeth McAlister, a professor at Wesleyan University who studies religion in Haiti.

Voodoo practitioners, most of whom are also Roman Catholic, congregate in Souvenance, Haiti, on Easter weekend 2010. (© **AP Images/ Jorge Saenz.**)

"We know that once night falls, the response of the population, which is camping out on the streets, is to sing hymns and pray. That tells us right away the response has been an intense reaching out to the spiritual," said McAlister.

Tragedies Cause an Uptick in Religious Fervor

When previous tragedies hit the island nation, including four back-to-back hurricanes in 2008, there was an uptick in religious fervor, and the increased conversion to charismatic forms of Protestantism has tracked with the country's modern political and natural disasters since the 1970s.

This soon after the earthquake, McAlister said Haitians are principally concerned with search and rescue efforts, but the conditions there both support and hinder some religious rituals, particularly voodoo.

"It is easier to do Christian prayers on the spot than conduct voodoo rituals," McAlister said. "Voodoo usually takes more time and the rituals are more elaborate."

Like Christianity, voodoo is monotheistic, but the incorporation of pagan practices—including the use of spells and spirit worship—has put it at odds with some traditional Christians.

Lacking a centralized hierarchy, voodoo's religious leaders can be women or men, known as hougans, who often create communities of followers that meet in small temples. Many rituals include dancing to drums and the sacrifice of animals, like chickens and goats. In some rituals, including one intended to heal the sick, the blood of a goat is consumed.

But voodoo houses of worship also serve roles familiar to those who practice Western religions.

"Most voodoo temples in Port-au-Prince function as social-services agencies, medical centers, psychologists, and places for trade," said McAlister. "Voodoo priests and priestesses perform a function like social workers. Temples form imaginary families in which congregations are the children of priest and priestess, who are often charismatic local leaders."

> Some evangelical leaders . . . have used a centuries-old Haitian legend as justification for believing the country is in league with the devil.

Thus far, in the days after the devastating quake, public religious displays have been reserved. Haitian citizens meet on the streets—what Port-au-Prince resident Richard Morse, via Twitter, called the city's "new living rooms"—for makeshift prayer gatherings. . . .

A "Pact to the Devil"

American religious institutions are moving millions of dollars in aid to help Haiti, but some evangelical leaders,

Religion in Haiti

The official state religion is Catholicism, but over the last four decades Protestant missionary activity has reduced the proportion of people who identify themselves as Catholic from over 90 percent in 1960 to less than 70 percent in 2000.

Haiti is famous for its popular religion, known to its practitioners as "serving the *lwa*" but referred to by the literature and the outside world as voodoo (*vodoun*). This religious complex is a syncretic mixture of African and Catholic beliefs, rituals, and religious specialists, and its practitioners (*sèvitè*) continue to be members of a Catholic parish. Long stereotyped by the outside world as "black magic," *vodoun* is actually a religion whose specialists derive most of their income from healing the sick rather than from attacking targeted victims.

Many people have rejected voodoo, becoming instead *katolik fran* ("unmixed Catholics" who do not combine Catholicism with service to the *lwa*) or *levanjil* (Protestants). The common claim that all Haitians secretly practice voodoo is inaccurate. Catholics and Protestants generally believe in the existence of *lwa*, but consider them demons to be avoided rather than family spirits to be served. The percentage of those who explicitly serve the family *lwa* is unknown but probably high.

Aside from the priests of the Catholic Church and thousands of Protestant ministers, many of them trained and supported by evangelical missions from the United States, informal religious specialists proliferate. Most notable are the voodoo specialists known by various names in different regions (*houngan, bokò, gangan*) and referred to as *manbo* in the case of female specialists. (Females are viewed as having the same spiritual powers as males, though in practice there are more *houngan* than *manbo*.) There are also bush priests (*pè savann*) who read specific Catholic prayers at funerals and other ceremonial occasions, and *hounsi*, initiated females who serve as ceremonial assistants to the *houngan* or *manbo*. . . .

Beliefs concerning the afterlife depend on the religion of the individual. Strict Catholics and Protestants believe in the existence of reward or punishment after death. Practitioners of voodoo assume that the souls of all the deceased go to an abode "beneath the waters," that is often associated with *lafrik gine* ("L'Afrique Guinée," or Africa). Concepts of reward and punishment in the afterlife are alien to *vodoun*.

SOURCE. *Timothy T. Schwartz, "Haiti,"* Countries and Their Cultures, *ed. Carol R. Ember and Melvin Ember, vol. 2. New York: Macmillan Reference USA, 2001, pp. 967–978.*

like Robertson, have used a centuries-old Haitian legend as justification for believing the country is in league with the devil.

"You know, something happened a long time ago in Haiti. They got together and swore a pact to the devil," Robertson said on the Christian Broadcasting Network's [CBN] "700 Club" Wednesday.

"They said, 'We will serve you if you get us free from the French.' True story."

The comments sparked a backlash, with many accusing Robertson of implying that the Haitians were responsible for the earthquake.

A spokesman for Robertson's CBN tried to clarify the pastor host's comments, saying, "Dr. Robertson never stated that the earthquake was God's wrath.

"His comments were based on the widely discussed 1791 slave rebellion led by Boukman Dutty at Bois Caiman, where the slaves allegedly made a famous pact with the devil in exchange for victory over the French. This history, combined with the horrible state of the country, has led countless scholars and religious figures over the centuries to believe the country is cursed," CBN spokesman Chris Roslan said in a statement.

CHAPTER **3**

Personal Narratives

A Sixteen-Year-Old Boy Loses His Mother and Home

Plan International

In the following interview, a sixteen-year-old Haitian boy tells his story to Plan International, an international aid agency. He survived the earthquake along with one of his sisters. However, his mother and two other sisters died when their house collapsed. The boy now sleeps under a tree with his sister and does not know what to do. He has no money, no food, and no work. His only thought for the future is to find somewhere to sleep, get a tent, and find some food for himself and his sister.

Photo on previous page: A woman displaced by the earthquake stands with her child outside a tent in a camp set up in a former Port-au-Prince, Haiti, golf club. (© Klavs Bo Christensen/Getty Images.)

Johnny [not his real name], who lost his mother and 2 sisters in the Haiti earthquake, shares his story of struggle to find shelter, get money and go to school. He has now received a tent and other vital supplies as part of Plan's[1] emergency relief work in Haiti.

My name is Johnny, I am 16 years old. I like playing basketball. I always used to laugh and enjoyed running around playing with people.

I was at home when the earthquake occurred. I was outside and was trying to go into the house again, but people were saying, "don't go in the house again because your mother is already dead. I don't want you to die." So I listened to them.

I have 3 sisters—2 of them died and one survived. Her name is Blandine, she is 13 years old. Now it's just me and my sister.

Somewhere to Sleep

My sister and I now go to sleep behind a tree. I don't have dreams. We have both been sick. My sister makes tea for me but I have to ask people for food or some money to buy food. Some people tell me a bad word that I can't

A young man carries wooden crosses to be placed at a memorial on the mass grave on the outskirts of Port-au-Prince, Haiti, on the first anniversary of the earthquake. (© Joe Raedle/Getty Images.)

repeat. Some people tell me to go away before they kick my butt. I tell them: "You don't know what you're saying."

I just walk away and go somewhere to cry.

> "I would like somewhere to sleep—and for God to bless me."

What do I want for the future? I would like somewhere to sleep—and for God to bless me. I need money to buy a tent and to eat with my sister. My clothes and phone are still in my house, so I have no clothes to wear. I have no tennis shoes.

I won't go back to the house to get these things because my mother is in the room with my other sisters and I don't want to find them.

No Food, No Job, No Money

My school is still there but I can't go because I have no money to go to school. The school asks me for money but I don't have a job or any money. I ask people if they have jobs, but they swear at me and tell me there are no jobs here because there are too many people.

We keep seeing the planes. What they bring, I don't know, maybe food boxes, water and maybe a tent. I try to see if I can help with the unloading. I'm going to see if I can get a tent and put it up near the tree where I sleep. It should help me sleep better than I have been at least.

I feel bad because a lot of houses were destroyed. A lot of people are dying. There is no food, no work, nothing. When I felt the earthquake, I cried because it was the first time I had experienced one. I was so scared that I just ran and ran. When I try to sleep, I think about that and I pray to God to not let this happen to us again.

Note

1. Plan International is a child development organization.

A US Graduate Student Is Trapped in Wreckage

Laura Wagner

In the following viewpoint, US student Laura Wagner describes her life in Haiti while she conducted research for her doctoral dissertation. She wants to commemorate that life because the people she knew, and who were very kind to her, are now dead. She tells the story of the earthquake, the collapse of the house in which she lived, and being trapped in wreckage with her Haitian friend crushed to death near her. Immediately after the earthquake, she was treated with compassion and generosity. Now she feels helpless and unable to do anything for the Haitians, except to tell their story.

I was sitting barefoot on my bed, catching up on ethnographic field notes, when the earthquake hit. As a child of the San Francisco area, I was underwhelmed at first. "An earthquake. This is unexpected," I thought.

SOURCE. Laura Wagner, "Haiti: A Survivor's Story," *Salon*, February 2, 2010. This article first appeared in Salon.com, at www.salon.com. An online version remains in the Salon archives. Reprinted with permission.

But then the shaking grew stronger. I had never felt such a loss of control, not only of my body but also of my surroundings, as though the world that contained me were being crumpled.

> I was surprised to die in this way, but not afraid. And then I was surprised not to be dead after all.

I braced myself in a doorway between the hallway and the kitchen, trying to hold on to the frame, and then a cloud of darkness and cement dust swallowed everything as the house collapsed. I was surprised to die in this way, but not afraid. And then I was surprised not to be dead after all. I was trapped, neither lying down nor sitting, with my left arm crushed between the planks of the shattered doorway and my legs pinned under the collapsed roof. Somewhere, outside, I heard people screaming, praying and singing. It was reassuring. It meant the world hadn't ended.

Before the Earthquake, Life Was Normal

I want you to know that, before the earthquake, things in Haiti were normal. Outside Haiti, people only hear the worst—tales that are cherry-picked, tales that are exaggerated, tales that are lies. I want you to understand that there was poverty and oppression and injustice in Port-au-Prince, but there was also banality. There were teenage girls who sang along hilariously with the love ballads of Marco Antonio Solís, despite not speaking Spanish. There were men who searched in vain for odd jobs by day and told never-ending Bouki and Ti Malis [Haitian folk] stories and riddles as the sun went down and rain began to fall on the banana leaves. There were young women who painted their toenails rose for church every Sunday, and stern middle-aged women who wouldn't let me leave the house without admonishing me to iron my skirt and comb my hair. There were young students who washed their uniforms and white socks every evening by hand, rhythmically working the detergent into a noisy foam. There were great water trucks that passed through the streets several times a day, inexplicably playing a squealing, mechanical version of the theme from "Titanic," which we all learned to ignore the same way we tuned out the overzealous and confused roosters that crowed at 3 A.M. There were families who finished each day no further ahead than they had begun it and then, at night, sat on the floor and intently followed the Mexican telenovelas dubbed into French. Their eyes trained on fantastic visions of alternate worlds in which roles become reversed and the righteous are rewarded, dreaming ahead into a future that might, against all odds, hold promise.

I need to tell you these things, not just so that you know, but also so I don't forget.

Under the Rubble

I think I was under the rubble for about two hours. Buried somewhere in what had been the kitchen, a mobile phone had been left to charge, and now it kept ringing. The ringtone was sentimental, the chorus of a pop love song. There was something sticky and warm on my shirt. I thought it was *sòs pwa*, a Haitian bean soup eaten over rice, which we'd had for lunch. I thought it was funny, that *sòs pwa* was leaking out of the overturned refrigerator and all over me. I thought, "When I get out, I will have to tell Melise about this." Melise was the woman who lived and worked in the house. I spent a large part of every day with her and her family—gossiping and joking, polishing the furniture with vegetable oil, cooking over charcoal and eating pounded breadfruit with our hands. She said my hands were soft. Her palms were so hard and calloused from a lifetime of household work that she could lift a hot pot with her bare hands. She called me her third daughter. I thought Melise would laugh to see me drenched in her *sòs pwa* from the bottom hem of my shirt up through my bra. It took me some time to figure out that what I thought was *sòs pwa* was actually my blood. I wrung it out of my shirt with my free right hand. I couldn't tell where it was coming from.

Melise did not make it out of the house. She died, we assume, at the moment of collapse. According to others, who told me later, she cried out, "Letènel, oh letènel!" and that was all. (The word is Creole for the French "l'Eternal," a cry out to God.) "She had been folding laundry on the second floor—the floor that crumbled onto the first floor, where I was pinned, thinking wildly of *sòs pwa*. Melise worked and lived in that house for 15 years. She dreamed of one day having her own home and being free. She talked about it all the time. She died in the wreckage of a place she did not consider her home.

I want to write everything down—those mundane remembrances of how life was before—because as time passes I am afraid that people will become fossilized, that their lives and identities will begin to be knowable only through the facts of their deaths. My field notes are buried in that collapsed house. Those notes are an artifact, a record of a lost time, stories about people when they were just people—living, ordinary people who told dirty jokes, talked one-on-one to God, blamed a fart on the cat, and made their way through a life that was grinding but not without joy or humor, or normality. I don't want my friends to be canonized.

Haitians Are Fiercely Generous

I had been in Port-au-Prince for a total of six months, conducting research on household workers and human rights. As a young American woman not affiliated with any of the large organizations that dominate the Haitian landscape, I was overwhelmed every day by the fierce generosity of Haitians. People who had little were eager to share their food, their homes, their time, their lives.

Now I'm cobbling together this narrative—these non-consecutive remembrances—in surreal and far-removed settings: first a hospital bed in South Miami, then a Cinnabon-scented airport terminal, now a large public university during basketball season. I can't do anything for those same people who gave of themselves so naturally and unflinchingly. My friends, who for months insisted on sharing whatever food they had made, even if I had already eaten, promising me "just a little rice" but invariably giving more. My friends, who walked me to the taptap stop nearly every day.

Now that the first journalistic burst has ended, now that the celebrity telethons have wrapped, the stories you hear are of "looters" and "criminals" set loose on a postapocalyptic wasteland. This is the same story that has always been told about Haiti, for more than 200 years, since the slaves had the temerity to not want to be slaves anymore. This is the same trope of savagery that has been used to strip Haiti and Haitians of legitimacy since the Revolution. But at the moment of the quake, even as the city and, for all we knew, the government collapsed, Haitian society did not fall into Hobbesian[1] anarchy. This stands in contradiction both to what is being shown on the news right now, and everything we assume about societies in moments of breakdown.

In the aftermath of the earthquake, there was great personal kindness and sacrifice, grace and humanity in the midst of natural and institutional chaos and rupture. My friend Frenel, who worked cleaning and maintaining the house, appeared within minutes to look for survivors. He created a passage through the still-falling debris using only a flashlight and a small hammer—the kind you would use to nail a picture to a wall. Completely trapped, the nerves in my left arm damaged, I could not help him save me. He told me, calmly, "Pray, Lolo, you must pray," as he broke up the cement and pulled it out, piece by piece, to free me. Once I was out, he gave me the sandals off his own feet. As I write this, I am still wearing them. At the United Nations compound, where Frenel ultimately guided and left me, everyone sat together on the cracked asphalt, bleeding and dazed, holding hands and praying as the aftershocks came. A little boy who had arrived alone trembled on my lap. Another family huddled under the same metallic emergency blanket with us. Their child looked at me, warily—a foreigner, covered in blood and dusted white with cement powder. His grandmother told him, "Ou mèt chita. Li malad, menm jan avek nou." You can sit. She's sick, too, just like us.

> In every calamity, it is inevitably the poor who suffer more, die more, and will continue to suffer and die after the cameras turn their gaze elsewhere.

Catastrophes Do Not Affect People Equally

Social scientists who study catastrophes say there are no natural disasters. In every calamity, it is inevitably the poor who suffer more, die more, and will continue to suffer and die after the cameras turn their gaze elsewhere. Do not be deceived by claims that everyone was affected equally—fault lines are social as well as geological. After all, I am here, with my white skin and my U.S. citizenship, listening to birds outside the window in the gray-brown of a North Carolina winter, while the people who welcomed me into their lives are still in Port-au-Prince, within the wreckage, several of them still not accounted for.

As I sat waiting to be flown out, trying to convince myself that I was just another injured person using up scant food and resources, a non-Haitian man whom I presumed worked for the U.N. approached me.

"Can you do me a favor?" he asked. "Could you write something down?"

I nodded, and he handed me a pen and paper.

"Tear the paper in half, and on the first half write 'unidentified local female' in block letters. Then on the second piece of paper write the same thing."

I looked up. There were bodies loaded into the back of a pickup truck. The woman's floral print dress was showing and her feet were hanging out. There were not enough sheets and blankets for the living patients, never mind enough to adequately wrap the dead. The U.N. guy looked at me and sort of smiled as I numbly tore the paper and wrote.

"After all, you need something to do. All the bars are closed," he said.

I stared at the bodies on the truck, and I hated him. I did not know which, if any, of my friends had survived. I imagined the people I love—Marlène, one of my best friends, or Damilove, the mother of my goddaughter—wrapped up in some scrap of cloth with their feet hanging out and some asshole tagging them with a half-piece of scrap paper that says they are anonymous, without history, unknown.

Haitians Are Suffering

I am telling you two things that seem contradictory: that people in Haiti are suffering horribly, and that Haitians are not sufferers in some preordained way. What I mean is that suffering is not some intrinsic aspect of Haitian existence, it is not something to get used to. The dead were once human beings with complex lives, and those in agony were not always victims.

In Haiti I was treated with incredible warmth and generosity by people who have been criminalized, condemned, dehumanized and abstractly pitied. They helped me in small, significant ways for the six months I was there, and in extraordinary ways in the hours after the quake. Now I cannot help them. I cannot do anything useful for them from here, except to employ the only strategy that was available to us all when we were buried in collapsed houses, listening to the frantic stirrings of life aboveground: to shout and shout until someone responds.

Note

1. Thomas Hobbes (1588–1679), an English philosopher, wrote in his best known work, *Leviathan*, that people live brutish existences and are naturally in a state of constant warfare.

A Haitian Man Tells the Story of the Earthquake by Telephone

Ferero Dessources, interviewed by Seth Daniel

In the following viewpoint, radio broadcaster Ferero Dessources tells the story of the Haiti earthquake to his brother-in-law, newspaper reporter Seth Daniel. Dessources was watching television in his living room when everything began to quake. Dessources describes scenes of total terror, and says that at the time of the interview, people were still afraid of aftershocks. As a radio broadcaster, he is working to help family members reconnect with each other. He also pleads for prayers, food, and water.

I t was a hot evening in Haiti's tropical capital of Port-au-Prince last Tuesday, January 12, [2010]. Scenes of "total terror" were the last thing on anyone's mind. Most who work were just arriving home. Others were preparing dinner in the way that those in Haiti do, most of the time over a fire—doing everything by hand—with fresh ingredients just purchased earlier at an outdoor market.

Ferero Dessources was watching television in his living room, his children and wife in another part of his house, which is in the Port-au-Prince neighborhood of Delmas.

> It was totally quiet at first because we've experienced nothing like that before.

Suddenly, there was an odd and violent shaking and everything that everyone had ever known in Haiti changed forever.

Dessources (who, for disclosure purposes, is this writer's brother-in-law) said the shaking lasted for what seemed like 10 seconds—though it was actually longer.

No one, initially, knew what was going on. It was as foreign an experience as a snowstorm.

A Terrible Silence

The 7.3 magnitude quake gave birth to a horrible silence, he said, one that soon erupted into chaos.

"We didn't say anything at first," he said, speaking by telephone from his home in Delmas, Haiti on Tuesday night. "It was totally quiet at first because we've experienced nothing like that before. Later, everyone started crying and screaming. I heard voices saying, 'Mama, mama!' It was hard to tell if people were crying from being in pain or because they were scared. It was probably both."

Dessources's home stayed its ground, but others in his neighborhood were not as lucky.

"In my neighborhood, a house collapsed and seven family members died," he said.

In the ensuing chaos and screaming, Dessources said that people took to the streets. They were running, crying and screaming.

No one knew what was going on.

There were people hurt.

But no one knew why.

Dessources works for one of the largest radio stations in Port-au-Prince, Signal FM, and he said that his first reaction was to call into work to see if they knew anything.

"Outside there was just screaming and I saw everyone running around and they were very scared," he said. "I kept asking everyone, 'What's going on. What's going on.' I called the station and they were talking to me and in the middle of the conversation, we just got cut. That's when I knew it was bad because communication had stopped."

The following night and the days afterward were something that Dessources was not able to put into colorful words, perhaps too horrible to recount.

Total Terror

"It was total terror, total terror," he said. "We've never seen anything like this. The people thought that there was going to be another bigger earthquake and they still do now. It's like post-traumatic stress. People are still waiting for another big earthquake. They all think another is coming at any moment. That's why they're still sleeping outside and won't go inside."

He also said that there is no exaggeration in the accounts broadcast on the network news. Things are as bad as reported. He said that some neighborhoods—such as his own—weathered the quake better than others. Many, though, were reduced to nothing.

That left people wandering the streets, trying to pick up the pieces, still trying to figure out what happened. In many cases, those outside Haiti—he said—knew more about the disaster than those who had lived through it.

Dessources and Signal FM, though, played an important part in helping people in the initial stages. The station was the only one that was able to broadcast out of

Port-au-Prince after the quake. Right now, it is still the only Haitian station on the air.

"It wasn't until the next day that we heard of the Presidential Palace falling and the extent of the disaster," he said. "There was no communication, but little by little there was information coming in. The palace and other information like that wasn't important to anyone, though. No one cared. People's lives were more important. Everyone was thinking about family members. Buildings were of little importance at that moment."

Mostly, he said, the night of the quake people prayed that it wouldn't rain.

"Tuesday night was the worst night of all for everyone," he said. "We were afraid it would rain. No one wanted to go into the houses because if it rained, those still standing might fall down too. Rain would have made it so much worse."

Trying to Help

Dessources said he and the radio staff have worked endlessly for the last week as people have lined up outside the station trying to find out what happened, trying in vain to get help for family members who were hurt, dying or already dead. It was an endless stream of shell-shocked people.

"Everybody was coming to us," he said. "They were lost, or looking for people. Most were trying to get help. Everyone had someone who was injured or dying. Some were just trying to make sense of it. We had to stay on the air because everyone was coming to us for help. It wasn't like work though. We were helping, not working. Everyone was helping each other. In the last three days, I've been at the station less, but right after the earthquake we would be there 13 or 14 hours a day."

> "We need food; we're running out—and water," he said. "There is no food without water."

In America, the station was picked up by many Haitian American radio stations and broadcast for hours on end. For Haitian Americans, Dessources's station was the only link to information about family in Haiti. Haitian Americans from Miami to New York to Boston stayed glued to Signal FM for any information they could gather about people in their native country.

"Pray for Haiti, America"

Dessources said that right now they still need food and water—the basics.

"We need food; we're running out—and water," he said. "There is no food without water."

Most importantly, though, he said the country needed prayer—especially for those that have been left with no family alive and no place to live.

"Pray for Haiti America," he said. "There are a lot of families here suffering. They've lost everything and they're still very scared. There are families with just one person left. Pray for them especially."

Three Medics Describe Their Experience in Haiti

Betsy Fine, John McGlade, and Eric Holden

In the following viewpoint, three members of the New York City Medics organization share their experience providing aid in the aftermath of the Haiti earthquake. Doctor Betsy Fine recalls some of their earlier missions to Pakistan but says that Haiti was the most emotionally difficult mission. Emergency medical technician John McGlade describes the difficult journey getting to the disaster area. Physician assistant Eric Holden recounts how the field hospitals and aid stations were organized. All three describe the many difficulties of providing aid in the devastated country.

Dr. Betsy Fine's Story

In October 2005, I responded to an email from the Society of Adolescent Medicine requesting a doctor to go to Kashmir after a massive earthquake. Within a week or so, I flew to New York City and then on to Pakistan with a group of complete strangers—a fairly close-knit but somewhat ragtag group of veteran NYC paramedics, off on their own with no organizational backing. It was a crazy thing to do, but it was the start of some of the most rewarding experiences of my career and my life. How a family doc with a specialty in adolescent medicine fit in with a group of seasoned New York paramedics was and remains a little unclear. Somehow, even though our skills sets are very different, our basic belief that anyone can do something to help ties us together.

Though each trip with NYC Medics was very different—the first to remote Kashmir, Pakistan, a second to refugee camps for displaced mountain people in Garhi Habibullah, Pakistan, and most recently to one of the poorest and most densely populated cities on earth in Port-au-Prince, Haiti, my friends and colleagues work with the same energy, compassion and utmost respect. I marvel at how folks whose work is in tiny fragments of lives in emergencies were as connected to the patients as those of us who spend years in practice getting to know them. Not only patients, but the local staff, translators and community completely bond with this group. Four and a half years later, we still get emails from our friends in Pakistan.

> "Our work, though meaningful, felt like a drop in the ocean."

Personally, I found Haiti the most emotionally difficult of our missions. Our work, though meaningful, felt like a drop in the ocean—compared with the homelessness, poverty, and a lack of food and water heaped on top of illness and injury and unimaginable loss. It has really stayed with me daily when I turn on the tap, walk in my home or open my full refrigerator. I am constantly reminded how the people of Haiti are living. We had the amazing fortune to be welcomed by the people we came to help and by the activist community people who would be there after we left.

In the end, it really is all about connections—something my friends from NYC Medics are extraordinarily good at. As one patient said to our gentle friend Chris in Kashmir, "You have two hands, I have two hands . . . we are the same." Ultimately, this is the reward of our work, to share our humanity and to stand with each other in the face of sorrow and loss. I am ever so grateful to have been a part of that.

An Emergency Medical Technician's Entry into Haiti

Six members of NYC Medics "Team 3" met with Ruben Flores [director of Haiti Operations, NYC Medics Team] for coffee, ID cards and a briefing at John F. Kennedy Airport in New York City around 3:30 A.M. Eight hours later, we were on the ground in Santo Domingo [Dominican Republic] waiting for the rest of our team from California. A few short hours into the afternoon, we were on the way to the Haiti border, several hours to the west.

The roads were a maze of potholes and broken asphalt, and an inevitable flat tire held us up for over an hour while it was repaired. In the Dominican Republic (DR), a flat tire isn't a problem. However, having two flats is a big deal, so we had to get it repaired just in case it happened again.

The flat tire and hour delay put us at the border after 9 P.M.; it had closed at 7. After a discussion with the immigrations officer who was responsible for the border, she approved our crossing, since we were "diplomats," and they opened the border gates for us, but it was too soon to celebrate. We hadn't figured on the animosity between the Dominicans and Haitians.

As our van drove into the border crossing, the guard said something to our driver that caused him to stop and back up into the DR. It was obvious that he was very shaken. She had told him that he would be murdered by Haitian bandits if he proceeded to Port au Prince in the dark. He wasn't going any further that night.

Once we returned to the DR, we were stuck. They told us we would have to stay the night in the "no man's land" at the border crossing. After several hours of cajoling the DR border guards, they agreed to let the team proceed, but then told us they were unable to reopen the gate because the key went home with the immigrations official. Our only option was to leave our van and climb the gate between the DR and Haiti. After the sergeant of the guard rolled back the barbed wire, we scaled the eight-foot fence with our bags. There we stood in the pitch black of the Haitian side, with our ride from Port au Prince about 200 yards away at the Haitian check point.

> "Our only option was to leave our van and climb the gate between the [Dominican Republic] and Haiti."

After a brief skirmish with a pack of barking dogs, we met our drivers and were off to Port au Prince. We finally arrived at the Delmas Gate camp of the 82nd Airborne, the place where we would be stationed for our mission, around 2 A.M.—23 hours after meeting in New York. In another 5 hours, we would begin seeing our first patients.

A Physician Assistant's Story

In January of this year, I was fortunate to be invited to join the first response team sent by NYC Medics to Haiti following the earthquake there. Many public and private organizations, both from the U.S. and abroad, sent teams as well. Most of these teams were composed of physicians, surgeons and nurses seeking to replicate a field version of the hospital environment—what they knew

At a field hospital set up on the grounds of Haiti's international airport, a paramedic from Miami, Florida, cares for a young boy injured in the earthquake. Medics came from many different countries to help the victims. (© Chip Somodevilla/Getty Images.)

best. The vast majority of field hospitals were centered at the airport, with fewer throughout the communities of Port au Prince.

Some volunteers with these organizations never left their field hospitals or saw anything other than the area immediately surrounding the international airport. Unfortunately, many patients were unable to arrange transportation to these facilities and stayed in their home communities without receiving the care they so desperately needed. Patients with femur fractures, significant dehydration or a crushed pelvis can't walk to their nearest hospital to obtain care. A link in the chain was missing.

NYC Medics took another approach to this problem. As a team founded and led by EMS [emergency medical services] professionals, it is not surprising that their model was based on doing what EMS does best: finding patients where they are, regardless of their circumstances, and providing care where they live. To the best of my knowledge, the teams from NYC Medics were the only ones to walk through the tent cities, finding and stabilizing patients in the field and treating or transferring them as their needs required. Our teams certainly needed the services of surgeons at the field hospitals for some of our critical patients, but without the services we provided, these patients would never have reached definitive care.

We also ran a series of mobile clinics at several locations throughout the city in areas with the most damage that one to two weeks after the quake had yet to see their first medical provider. These were the "slums" of Port au Prince—areas like Citie Militaire and Citie Soleil that were considered "too dangerous to travel through." We traveled to these areas alone as a team and later with transportation assistance from the Army 82nd airborne, and it was where we found some of the most critically injured victims. Our clinics were set up in such a way that we could arrive at a location and be ready to see patients within a very short time. Most days we saw 400 or more patients using this model. As soon as we had seen everyone in a neighborhood, we packed up and moved on to other sites that we had scouted and discovered to be in need.

> We could arrive at a location and be ready to see patients within a very short time.

In future disasters, we need to remember one lesson: Disaster zones need skilled providers and support staff and all the skills they can provide in field hospitals, but they also need rapid response teams like those fielded by NYC Medics who can get to patients quickly where they live to provide care in the out-of-hospital environment and transportation for those with issues requiring more significant interventions.

CHRONOLOGY

2010

January 12   At approximately 4:53 p.m. local time, a magnitude 7.0 earthquake hits Haiti, its epicenter just sixteen miles from Port-au-Prince, Haiti's capital and most heavily populated area. With buildings collapsed and infrastructure undermined, estimates of deaths and damage vary wildly. At least 70 percent of the buildings in Port-au-Prince are destroyed.

January 13   Search and rescue teams from Cuba and Peru arrive, as does Doctors Without Borders, who sets up triage centers to help the injured. The US Coast Guard cutter *Forward* arrives at Port-au-Prince. The International Red Cross creates a website to help families regain contact with loved ones.

January 14   Rescue teams from at least twenty countries arrive in Haiti to continue the search and rescue effort. Bodies line the streets. Haitian officials and aid workers struggle to reestablish communication lines. Infrastructure damage delays relief efforts as many roads are completely blocked by debris.

January 15   Aid continues to pour in from around the world, with rescue workers and equipment arriving from France, Israel, and Canada. However, it is still difficult for workers to distribute aid to those in need because of the widespread chaos and destruction.

January 17   Haitian police fire on looters. It is difficult to determine if these are criminals raiding food supplies or residents becoming desperate for food and water.

Earthquake aftershocks continue, sending Haitians running out into the streets in fear.

US Naval and Coast Guard vessels are in the waters around Haiti to lend support.

January 18   US Marines arrive to begin a humanitarian disaster relief effort. The US Air Force begins to drop aid packages in the countryside where people have been cut off since January 12. US troops patrol streets and assume control of the airport in an attempt to restore order.

January 21   Many US ships are in Haitian harbors, as are Dutch and Spanish ships carrying supplies. Haitian workers are throwing bodies into mass graves as fear of contagion and cholera mount.

January 23   The Haitian government suspends rescue efforts. All missing persons are now assumed dead.

January 30   The World Food Programme, working with other relief organizations, begins a large food distribution program. Women with vouchers will be the only people eligible to receive food. The US military provides security for the distribution.

February 1   Ten US Baptist missionaries from Idaho are stopped as they attempt to move Haitian children they claim are orphans to the Dominican Republic for eventual adoption in the United States. The missionaries are charged with child trafficking and abduction.

February 8   The final survivor of the Haiti earthquake is found.

February 10 Haitian officials announce that more than 250,000 people have died and another 300,000 have been injured as a result of the quake. However, different officials offer conflicting totals of dead and injured, raising questions about the accuracy of the accounts.

February 12 US forces begin returning home, reducing the US military presence in Haiti from twenty thousand to thirteen thousand troops.

March 7 The remaining US troops prepare to leave Haiti.

June A study sponsored by the United States Agency for International Development argues that the death toll of the Haiti earthquake is forty-six thousand to eighty-five thousand dead, far lower than Haitian government officials reported.

October Reports of an increase in child trafficking in Haiti emerge in the aftermath of the earthquake.

October–December A major cholera outbreak in Haiti kills 3,500 people.

November Presidential elections are held in Haiti with inconclusive results, leading to civil unrest.

2011

January Former Haitian president Jean-Claude Duvalier returns to Haiti from exile and faces criminal charges of corruption.

One year after the earthquake, large sections of Port-au-Prince remain buried under rubble and thousands of residents made homeless by the quake continue to live in emergency tent cities.

FOR FURTHER READING

Books

Miriam Aronin, *Earthquake in Haiti*. New York: Bearport, 2011.

Edwidge Danticat, *Tent Life: Haiti*. Brooklyn, NY: Umbrage Editions, 2010.

Rachael A. Donlon, *Haiti: Earthquake and Response*. New York: Nova Science Publishers, 2012.

Paul Farmer and Joia Mukherjee, *Haiti After the Earthquake*. New York: PublicAffairs, 2011.

Martin Munro, *Haiti Rising: Haitian History, Culture and the Earthquake of 2010*. Kingston, Jamaica: University of the West Indies Press, 2010.

Sandra Marquez Stathis, *Rubble: The Search for a Haitian Boy*. Guildford, CN: Lyons Press, 2012.

Editors of *Time* magazine, *Haiti: Tragedy and Hope*. New York: Time Books, 2010.

Susan Magnuson Walsh, *Walking in Broken Shoes: A Nurse's Story about Haiti and the Earthquake*. Larkspur, CO: Grace Acres Press, 2011.

Jesse Joshua Watson, *Hope for Haiti*. New York: G.P. Putnam's Sons, 2010.

Periodicals and Internet Sources

Nicholas Ambraseys and Roger Bilham, "Corruption Kills: On the Anniversary of Haiti's Devastating Quake, Nicholas Ambraseys and Roger Bilham Calculate That 83% of All Deaths from Building Collapse in Earthquakes over the Past 30 Years Occurred in Countries That Are Anomalously Corrupt," *Nature*, vol. 469, no. 7329, January 13, 2011.

"Americans Rush to Adopt Orphaned Haitian Children," *Today MSNBC*, January 20, 2010. today.msnbc.com.

Randal C. Archibold, "U.S. Reduces Estimates of Homeless in Haiti Quake," *New York Times*, May 31, 2011. www.nytimes.com.

Marisol Bello, "Haiti Survivors Continue to Rebuild Lives," *USA Today*, May 13, 2011.

"Building a Better Future for Haiti," *Futurist*, vol. 45, no. 3, May–June 2011.

"Frustration Sets In: Haiti's Earthquake," *Economist*, vol. 396, no. 8693, July 31, 2010.

Mac McClelland, "Fact-Checking Haiti's Death Toll," *Mother Jones*, June 1, 2011. www.motherjones.com.

Barack Obama, "We Can't Wait: The Time to Act Is Now," WhiteHouse.gov, January 14, 2010. www.whitehouse.gov.

Georgianne Nienaber, "Flawed Earthquake Report a Bullwhip on the Backs of Haitians," *LA Progressive*, June 1, 2011. www.laprogressive.com.

Michael Petrou, "Fleeing the Capital: Thousands Stream Out of Port-au-Prince, But the Hope of Rebuilding Remains," *Maclean's*, vol. 123, no. 4, February 8, 2010.

Tom Price, "The Other Haiti: Rebuilding Quake-Shattered Lives Beyond Port-au-Prince," *America*, vol. 203, no. 10, October 18, 2010.

Janet Reitman, "Beyond Relief: How the World Failed Haiti," *Rolling Stone*, August 4, 2011.

"Report Challenges Haiti Earthquake Death Toll," *BBC News*, June 1, 2011. www.bbc.co.uk.

Bonnie Rocheman, "Breast-Milk for Haiti: Why Donations Are Being Discouraged," *Time*, January 29, 2010. www.time.com.

Paul Shirley, "If You Rebuild It, They Will Come," *Flip Collective*, January 26, 2010. www.flipcollective.com.

Pete Spotts, "Risk of Fresh Haiti Earthquake Greater Than Thought," *Christian Science Monitor*, January 12, 2011.

Tracey Wilkinson, "Rape Flourishes in Rubble of Haitian Earthquake," *Los Angeles Times*, February 4, 2011. www.latimes.com.

Websites

CNN: Haiti Earthquake (edition.cnn.com/SPECIALS/2010/haiti.quake). The Cable News Network's special site focusing on the Haiti earthquake provides video, photographs, and personal narratives as well as straight forward reporting on the event. The site also includes updated reports evaluating the ongoing effects of the earthquake on Haiti.

Disaster Emergency Committee (www.dec.uk.org). The Disaster Emergency Committee is an organization that brings together aid agencies across the United Kingdom to provide aid for people affected by disasters in developing nations. On this site, facts and figures concerning the Haiti earthquake provide continuously updated information about the aftermath of the earthquake as well as archival material concerning Haiti before the quake.

The United States Geological Survey (www.usgs.gov). The United States Geological Survey's Earthquake Hazards Program is responsible for monitoring, researching, and reporting earthquakes. The site has an abundance of information about earthquakes in general and about the Haiti earthquake in particular, including archival articles reporting on the earthquake as it happened and later articles evaluating the effects.

INDEX

US military and, 43
vigilantes and, 43
Volcy, Assad, 80
Voodoo (vodoun), 130, *131*, 132, 133

W

Wagner, Laura, 139–146
Wesleyan University, 131
WFP (World Food Programme), 103–108

WHO (World Health Organization), 103–108
Women's Refugee Commission, 112
World Bank, 67*t*, 124
World Vision, 82

Z

Zimmerman, Robert, 27
Zoe's Ark, 113–114